ISBN 0-8373-4050-0

C-4050   CAREER EXAMINATION SERIES

This is your
PASSBOOK® for...

Employee Benefits Representative

Test Preparation Study Guide

Questions & Answers

NLC

NATIONAL LEARNING CORPORATION

Copyright © 2005 by

National Learning Corporation

212 Michael Drive, Syosset, New York 11791

(516) 921-8888
Outside N.Y.: 1(800) 645-6337
ORDER FAX: 1(516) 921-8743
www.passbooks.com
email: passbooks @ aol.com
sales @ passbooks.com
info @ passbooks.com

PRINTED IN THE UNITED STATES OF AMERICA

PASSBOOK®

NOTICE

PASSBOOK SERIES®

THE *PASSBOOK SERIES*® has been created to prepare applicants and candidates for the ultimate academic battlefield—the examination room.

At some time in our lives, each and every one of us may be required to take an examination—for validation, matriculation, admission, qualification, registration, certification, or licensure.

Based on the assumption that every applicant or candidate has met the basic formal educational standards, has taken the required number of courses, and read the necessary texts, the *PASSBOOK SERIES*® furnishes the one special preparation which may assure passing with confidence, instead of failing with insecurity. Examination questions—together with answers—are furnished as the basic vehicle for study so that the mysteries of the examination and its compounding difficulties may be eliminated or diminished by a sure method.

This book is meant to help you pass your examination provided that you qualify and are serious in your objective.

The entire field is reviewed through the huge store of content information which is succinctly presented through a provocative and challenging approach—the question-and-answer method.

A climate of success is established by furnishing the correct answers at the end of each test.

You soon learn to recognize types of questions, forms of questions, and patterns of questioning. You may even begin to anticipate expected outcomes.

You perceive that many questions are repeated or adapted so that you gain acute insights, which may enable you to score many sure points.

You learn how to confront new questions, or types of questions, and to attack them confidently and work out the correct answers.

You note objectives and emphases, and recognize pitfalls and dangers, so that you may make positive educational adjustments.

Moreover, you are kept fully informed in relation to new concepts, methods, practices, and directions in the field.

You discover that you are actually taking the examination all the time: you are preparing for the examination by "taking" an examination, not by reading extraneous and/or supererogatory textbooks.

In short, this PASSBOOK®, used directedly, should be an important factor in helping you to pass your test.

EMPLOYEE BENEFITS REPRESENTATIVE

DUTIES
Coordinates benefits programs particular to the city such as life and health insurance,
credit union systems, pension plans, tax deferred annuity, worker's compensation, etc.;
maintains personnel files and updates said files with appropriate documents; conducts
orientation/benefits interviews with new employees to discuss fringe benefits; acts as
liaison with various benefit agencies and the department concerning clarification of
policies, procedures and plan updates; maintains personnel files in connection with the
jurisdiction's fringe benefits and compensation programs; assists retirees in the
application and processing of retirement benefits and medical benefits; compiles bills
and charges to carriers, as well as directs premium billing to employees; assures that
effective claims management procedures are in effect; assists employees interested in
the credit union system by giving assistance in processing forms, applications and
related requirements; may perform the duties of civil service secretary.

SCOPE OF THE EXAMINATION
The written test will cover knowledge, skills and/or abilities in such areas as:

1. Interviewing;
2. Office record keeping;
3. Preparing written material; and
4. Understanding and interpreting written material based on laws, policies and
   procedures relating to health insurance and retirement.

HOW TO TAKE A TEST

I. YOU MUST PASS AN EXAMINATION

A. *WHAT EVERY CANDIDATE SHOULD KNOW*

Examination applicants often ask us for help in preparing for the written test. What can I study in advance? What kinds of questions will be asked? How will the test be given? How will the papers be graded?

As an applicant for a civil service examination, you may be wondering about some of these things. Our purpose here is to suggest effective methods of advance study and to describe civil service examinations.

Your chances for success on this examination can be increased if you know how to prepare. Those "pre-examination jitters" can be reduced if you know what to expect. You can even experience an adventure in good citizenship if you know why civil service examinations are given.

B. *WHY ARE CIVIL SERVICE EXAMINATIONS GIVEN?*

Civil service examinations are important to you in two ways. As a citizen, you want public jobs filled by employees who know how to do their work. As a job-seeker, you want a fair chance to compete for that job on an equal footing with other candidates. The best known means of accomplishing this two-fold goal is the competitive examination.

Examinations are widely publicized throughout the nation. They may be administered for jobs in federal, state, city, municipal, town, or village governments or agencies.

Any citizen may apply, with some limitations, such as the age or residence of applicants. Your experience and education may be reviewed to see whether you meet the requirements for the particular examination. When these requirements exist, they are reasonable and are applied consistently to all applicants. Thus, a competitive examination may cause you some uneasiness now, but it is your privilege and safeguard.

C. *HOW ARE CIVIL SERVICE EXAMINATIONS DEVELOPED?*

Examinations are carefully written by trained technicians who are specialists in the field known as "psychological measurement," in consultation with recognized authorities in the field of work that the test will cover. These experts recommend the subject matter areas or skills to be tested; only those knowledges or skills important to your success on the job are included. The most reliable books and source materials available are used as references. Together, the experts and technicians judge the difficulty level of the questions.

Test technicians know how to phrase questions so that the problem is clearly stated. Their ethics do not permit "trick" or "catch" questions. Questions may have been tried out on sample groups, or subjected to statistical analysis, to determine their usefulness.

Written tests are often used in combination with performance tests, ratings of training and experience, and oral interviews. All of these measures combine to form the best known means of finding the right man for the right job.

II. HOW TO PASS THE WRITTEN TEST

A. *NATURE OF THE EXAMINATION*

To prepare intelligently for civil service examinations, you should know how they differ from school examinations you have taken. In school you were assigned certain definite pages to read or subjects to cover. The examination questions were quite detailed and usually emphasized memory. Civil service examinations, on the other hand, try to discover your present ability to perform the duties of a position, plus your potentiality to learn these duties. In other words, a civil service examination attempts to predict how successful you will be. Questions cover such a broad area that they cannot be as minute and detailed as school examination questions.

In the public service similar kinds of work, or positions, are grouped together in one "class." This process is known as "position-classification." All the positions in a class are paid according to the salary range for that class. One class title covers all these positions, and they are all tested by the same examination.

B. *FOUR BASIC STEPS*

1. Study the Announcement.--How, then, can you know what subjects to study? Our best answer is: "Learn as much as possible about the class of positions for which you have applied." The examination will test the knowledge, skills, and abilities needed to do the work.

Your most valuable source of information about the position you want is the official announcement of the examination. This announcement lists the training and experience qualifications. Check these standards and apply only if you come reasonably close to meeting them.

The brief description of the position in the examination announcement offers some clues to the subjects which will be tested. Think about the job itself. Review the duties in your mind. Can you perform them, or are there some in which you are rusty? Fill in the blank spots in your preparation.

Many jurisdictions preview the written test in the examination announcement by including a section called "Knowledge and Abilities Required," "Scope of Examination," or some similar heading. Here you will find out specifically what fields will be tested.

2. Review Your Own Background.-- Once you learn in general what the position is all about, and what you need to know to do the work, ask yourself which subjects you already know fairly well and which need improvement. You may wonder whether to concentrate on improving your strong areas or on building some background in your fields of weakness. When the announcement has specified "some knowledge" or "considerable knowledge," or has used adjectives such as "beginning principles of ...." or "advanced .....methods," you can get a clue as to the number and difficulty of questions to be asked in any given field. More questions, and hence broader coverage, would be included for those subjects which are more important in the work. Now weigh your strengths and weaknesses against the job requirements and prepare accordingly.

3. Determine the Level of the Position.-- Another way to tell how intensively you should prepare is to understand the level of the job for which you are applying. Is it the entering level? In other words, is this the position in which beginners in a field of work are hired? Or is it an intermediate or advanced level? Sometimes this is indicated by such words as "Junior" or "Senior" in the class title.Other jurisdictions use Roman numerals to designate the level: Clerk I,

Clerk II, for example. The word "Supervisor" sometimes appears in the title. If the level is not indicated by the title, check the description of duties. Will you be working under very close supervision, or will you have responsibility for independent decisions in this work?

4. Choose Appropriate Study Materials.-- Now that you know the subjects to be examined and the relative amount of each subject to be covered, you can choose suitable study materials. For beginning level jobs, or even advanced ones, if you have a pronounced weakness in some aspect of your training, read a modern, standard textbook in that field. Be sure it is up-to-date and has general coverage. Such books are normally available at your library, and the librarian will be glad to help you locate one. For entry level positions, questions of appropriate difficulty are chosen -- neither highly advanced questions, nor those too simple. Such questions require careful thought but not advanced training.

If the position for which you are applying is technical or advanced, you will read more advanced, specialized material. If you are already familiar with the basic principles of your field, elementary textbooks would waste your time. Concentrate on advanced textbooks and technical periodicals. Think through the concepts and review difficult problems in your field.

These are all general sources. You can get more ideas on your own initiative, following these leads. For example, training manuals and publications of the government agency which employs workers in your field can be useful, particularly for technical and professional positions. A letter or visit to the government department involved may result in more specific study suggestions, and certainly will provide you with a more definite idea of the exact nature of the position you are seeking.

II. KINDS OF TESTS

Tests are used for purposes other than measuring knowledge and ability to perform specified duties. For some positions, it is equally important to test ability to make adjustments to new situations or to profit from training. In others, basic mental abilities not dependent upon information are essential. Questions which test these things may not appear as pertinent to the duties of the position as those which test for knowledge and information. Yet they are often highly important parts of a fair examination. For very general questions, it is almost impossible to help you direct your study efforts. What we can do is to point out some of the more common of these general abilities needed in public service positions and describe some typical questions.

1. General Information

Broad, general information has been found useful for predicting job success in some kinds of work. This is tested in a variety of ways, from vocabulary lists to questions about current events. Basic background in some field of work, such as sociology or economics, may be sampled in a group of questions. Often these are principles which have become familiar to most persons through "exposure" rather than through formal training. It is difficult to advise you how to study for these questions; being alert to the world around you is our best suggestion.

2. Verbal Ability

An example of an ability needed in many positions is verbal or language ability. Verbal ability is, in brief, the ability to use and understand words. Vocabulary and grammar tests are typical measures of this ability. "Reading comprehension" or "paragraph interpretation" questions are common in many kinds of civil service tests. You are given a paragraph of written material and asked to find its central meaning.

3. Numerical Ability

Number skills can be tested by the familiar arithmetic problem, by checking paired lists of numbers to see which are alike and which are different, or by interpreting charts and graphs. In the latter test, a graph may be printed in the test booklet which you are asked to use as the basis for answering questions.

4. Observation

A popular test for law-enforcement positions is the observation test. A picture is shown to you for several minutes, then taken away. Questions about the picture test your ability to observe both details and larger elements.

5. Following Directions

In many positions in the public service, the employee must be able to carry out written instructions dependably and accurately. You may be given a chart with several columns, each column listing a variety of information. The questions require you to carry out directions involving the information given in the chart.

6. Skills and Aptitudes

Performance tests effectively measure some manual skills and aptitudes. When the skill is one in which you are trained, such as typing or shorthand, you can practice. These tests are often very much like those given in business school or high school courses. For many of the other skills and aptitudes, however, no short-time preparation can be made. Skills and abilities natural to you or that you have developed throughout your lifetime are being tested.

Many of the general questions just described provide all the data needed to answer the questions and ask you to use your reasoning ability to find the answers. Your best preparation for these tests, as well as for tests of facts and ideas, is to be at your physical and mental best. You, no doubt, have your own methods of getting into an exam-taking mood and keeping "in shape." The next section lists some ideas on this subject.

IV. KINDS OF QUESTIONS

Only rarely is the "essay" question, which you answer in narrative form, used in civil service tests. Civil service tests are usually of the short-answer type. Full instructions for answering these questions will be given to you at the examination. But in case this is your first experience with short-answer questions and separate answer sheets, here is what you need to know.

1. Multiple-Choice Questions

Most popular of the short-answer questions is the "multiple-choice" or "best-answer" question. It can be used, for example, to test for factual knowledge, ability to solve problems, or judgment in meeting situations found at work.

A multiple-choice question is normally one of three types:

(1) It can begin with an incomplete statement followed by several possible endings. You are to find the one ending which *best* completes the statement, although some of the others may not be entirely wrong.

(2) It can also be a complete statement in the form of a question which is answered by choosing one of the statements listed.

(3) It can be in the form of a problem -- again you select the best answer.

Here is an example of a multiple-choice question with a discussion which should give you some clues as to the method for choosing the right answer.

SAMPLE QUESTION:

When an employee has a complaint about his assignment, the action which will *best* help him overcome his difficulty is

    (A) to discuss his difficulty with his co-workers

    (B) to take the problem to the head of the organization

    (C) to take the problem to the person who gave him the assignment

    (D) to say nothing to anyone about his complaint

In answering this question you should study each of the choices to find which is best. Consider choice (A). Certainly an employee may discuss his complaint with fellow employees, but no change or improvement can result, and the complaint remains unsolved. Choice (B) is a poor choice since the head of the organization probably does not know what assignment you have been given, and taking your problem to him is known as "going over the head" of the supervisor. The supervisor, or person who made the assignment, is the person who can clarify it or correct any injustice. Choice (C) is, therefore, correct. To say nothing, as in choice (D), is unwise. Supervisors have an interest in knowing the problems employees are facing, and the employee is seeking a solution to his problem.

  2. True-False Questions

The "true-false" or "right-wrong" form of question is sometimes used. Here a complete statement is given. Your problem is to decide whether the statement is right or wrong.

SAMPLE QUESTION:

A person-to-person long distance telephone call costs less than a station-to-station call to the same city.

This question is wrong, or "false," since person-to-person calls are more expensive.

This is not a complete list of all possible question forms, although most of the others are variations of these common types. You will always get complete directions for answering questions. Be sure you understand *how* to mark your answers -- ask questions until you do.

V. RECORDING YOUR ANSWERS

For an examination with very few applicants, you may be told to record your answers in the test booklet itself. Separate answer sheets are much more common. If this separate answer sheet is to be scored by machine -- and this is often the case -- it is highly important that you mark your answers correctly in order to get credit.

An electric test-scoring machine is often used in civil service offices because of the speed with which papers can be scored. Machine-scored answer sheets must be marked with a special pencil, which will be given to you. This pencil has a high graphite content which responds to the electrical scoring machine. As a matter of fact, stray dots may register as answers, so do not let your pencil rest on the answer sheet while you are pondering the correct answer. Also, if your pencil lead breaks or is otherwise defective, ask for another.

Since the answer sheet will be dropped in a slot in the scoring machine, be careful not to bend the corners or get the paper crumpled.

The answer sheet normally has five vertical columns of numbers, with 30 numbers to a column. These numbers correspond to the question numbers in your test booklet. After each number, going across the page, are four or five pairs of dotted lines. These short dotted lines have small letters or numbers above them. The first two pairs may also have a "T" and "F" above the letters. This indicates that the first two pairs only are to be used if the questions are of the true-false type. If the questions are multiple-choice, disregard this "T" and "F" completely, and pay attention only to the small number or letters.

Answer your questions in the manner of the sample that follows. Proceed in the sequential steps outlined below.

Assume that you are answering question 32, which is:

32. The largest city in the United States is:
    A. Washington, D.C.   B. New York City   C. Chicago
    D. Detroit   E. San Francisco

1. Choose the answer you think is best.
    New York City is the largest, so choice B is correct.
2. Find the row of dotted lines numbered the same as the question you are answering.
    This is question number 32, so find row number 32.
3. Find the pair of dotted lines corresponding to the answer you have chosen.
    You have chosen answer B, so find the pair of dotted lines marked "B".
4. Make a solid black mark between the dotted lines.
    Go up and down two or three times with your pencil so plenty of graphite rubs off, but do not let the mark get outside or above the dots.

	T A	F B	C	D	E
29	⠿	⠿	⠿	⠿	⠿
30	⠿	⠿	⠿	⠿	⠿
31	⠿	⠿	⠿	⠿	⠿
32	⠿	▮	⠿	⠿	⠿
33	⠿	⠿	⠿	⠿	⠿

VI. BEFORE THE TEST

Common sense will help you find procedures to follow to get ready for an examination. Too many of us, however, overlook these sensible measures. Indeed, nervousness and fatigue have been found to be the most serious reasons why applicants fail to do their best on civil service tests. Here is a list of reminders.

1. Begin Your Preparation Early

Don't wait until the last minute to go scurrying around for books and materials or to find out what the position is all about.

2. Prepare Continuously

An hour a night for a week is better than an all-night cram session. This has been definitely established. What is more, a night a week for a month will return better dividends than crowding your study into a shorter period of time.

3. Locate the Place of the Examination

You have been sent a notice telling you when and where to report for the examination. If the location is in a different town or otherwise unfamiliar to you, it would be well to inquire the best route and learn something about the building.

4. Relax the Night Before the Test

Allow your mind to rest. Do not study at all that night. Plan some mild recreation or diversion; then go to bed early and get a good night's sleep.

5. Get Up Early Enough to Make a Leisurely Trip to the Place for the Test

Then unforeseen events, traffic snarls, unfamiliar buildings, will not upset you.

6. Dress Comfortably

A written test is not a fashion show. You will be known by number and not by name, so wear something comfortable.

7. Leave Excess Paraphernalia at Home

Shopping bags and odd bundles will get in your way. You need bring only the items mentioned in the official notice sent to you; usually everything you need is provided. Do not bring reference books to the examination. They will only confuse those last minutes and be taken away from you when in the test room.

8. Arrive Somewhat Ahead of Time

If because of transportation schedules you must get there very early, bring a newspaper or magazine to take your mind off yourself while waiting.

9. Locate the Examination Room

When you have found the proper room, you will be directed to the seat or part of the room where you will sit. Sometimes you are given a sheet of instructions to read while you are waiting. Do not fill out any forms until you are told to do so; just read them and be ready.

10. Relax and Prepare to Listen to the Instructions

11. If you have any physical problem that may keep you from doing your best, be sure to tell the test administrator. If you are sick, or in poor health, you really cannot do your best on the test. You can come back and take the test some other time.

I. AT THE TEST

The day of the test is here and you have the test booklet in your hand. The temptation to get going is very strong. Caution! There is more to success than knowing the right answers. You must know how to identify your papers and understand variations in the type of short-answer question used in this particular examination. Follow these suggestions for maximum results from your efforts:

1. Cooperate with the Monitor

The test administrator has a duty to create a situation in which you can be as much at ease as possible. He will give instructions, tell you when to begin, check to see that you are marking your answer sheet correctly. He is not there to guard you, although he will see that your competitors do not take unfair advantage. He wants to help you do your best.

2. Listen to All Instructions

Don't jump the gun! Wait until you understand all directions. In most civil service tests you get more time than you need to answer the questions. So don't get in a hurry. Read each word of instructions until you clearly understand the meaning. Study the examples. Listen to all announcements. Follow directions. Ask questions if you do not understand what to do.

3. Identify Your Papers

Civil service examinations are usually identified by number only. You will be assigned a number; you must not put your name on your test papers. Be sure to copy your number correctly. Since more than one examination may be given, copy your exact examination title.

4. Plan Your Time

Unless you are told that a test is a "speed" or "rate-of-work" test, speed itself is not usually important. Time enough to answer all the questions will be provided. But this does not mean that you have all day. An overall time limit has been set. Divide the total time (in minutes) by the number of questions to get the approximate time you have for each question.

5. Do Not Linger Over Difficult Questions

If you come across a difficult question, mark it with a paper clip (useful to have along) and come back to it when you have been through the booklet. One caution if you do this -- be sure to skip a number on your answer sheet too. Check often to be sure that you have not lost your place and that you are marking in the row numbered the same as the question you are answering.

6. Read the Questions

Be sure you know what the question asks! Many capable people are unsuccessful because they failed to *read* the questions correctly.

7. Answer All Questions

Unless you have been instructed that a penalty will be deducted for incorrect answers, it is better to guess than to omit a question.

8. Speed Tests

It is often better *not* to guess on speed tests. It has been found that on timed tests people are tempted to spend the last few seconds before time is called in marking answers at random -- without even reading them -- in the hope of picking up a few extra points. To discourage this practice, the instructions may warn you that your score will be "corrected" for guessing. That is, a penalty will be applied. The incorrect answers will be deducted from the correct ones, or some other penalty formula will be used.

9. Review Your Answers

If you finish before time is called, go back to the questions you guessed or omitted to give further thought to them. Review other answers if you have time.

10. Return Your Test Materials

If you are ready to leave before others have finished or time is called, take *all* your materials to the monitor and leave quietly. Never take any test material with you. The monitor can discover whose papers are not complete, and taking a test booklet may be grounds for disqualification.

II. EXAMINATION TECHNIQUES

1. Read the *general* instructions carefully. These are usually printed on the first page of the examination booklet. As a rule, these instructions refer to the timing of the examination; the fact that you should not start work until the signal and must stop work at a signal, etc. If there are any *special* instructions, such as a choice of questions to be answered, make sure that you note this instruction carefully.

2. When you are ready to start work on the examination, that is as soon as the signal has been given, read the instructions to each question booklet, underline any key words or phrases, such as *least, best, outline, describe*, and the like. In this way you will tend to answer as requested rather than discover on reviewing your paper that you *listed without describing*, that you selected the *worst* choice rather than the *best* choice, etc.

3. If the examination is of the objective or so-called multiple-choice type, that is, each question will also give a series of possible answers: A, B, C, or D, and you are called upon to select the best answer and write the letter next to that answer on your answer paper, it is advisable to start answering each question in turn. There may be anywhere from 50 to 100 such questions in the three or four hours allotted and you can see how much time would be taken if you read through all the questions before beginning to answer any. Furthermore, if you come across a question or a group of questions which you know would be difficult to answer, it would undoubtedly affect your handling of all the other questions.

4. If the examination is of the esssay-type and contains but a few questions, it is a moot point as to whether you should read all the questions before starting to answer any one. Of course if you are given a choice, say five out of seven and the like, then it is essential to read all the questions so you can eliminate the two which are most difficult. If, however, you are asked to answer all the questions, there may be danger in trying to answer the easiest one first because you may find that you will spend too much time on it. The best technique is to answer the first question, then proceed to the second, etc.

5. Time your answers. Before the examination begins, write down the time it started, then add the time allowed for the examination and write down the time it must be completed, then divide the time available somewhat as follows:

(a) If 3½ hours are allowed, that would be 210 minutes. If you have 80 objective-type questions, that would be an average of 2½ minutes per question. Allow yourself no more than 2 minutes per question, or a total of 160 minutes, which will permit about 50 minutes to review.

(b) If for the time allotment of 210 minutes, there are 7 essay questions to answer, that would average about 30 minutes a question. Give yourself only 25 minutes per question so that you have about 35 minutes to review.

6. The most important instruction is *to read each question* and make sure you know what is wanted. The second most important instruction is to *time yourself properly* so that you answer every question. The third most important instruction is to *answer every question*. Guess if you have to but include something for each question. Remember that you will receive no credit for a blank and will probably receive some credit if you write something in answer to an essay question. If you guess a letter, say "B" for a multiple-choice question, you may have guessed right. If you leave a blank as the answer to a multiple-choice question, the examiners may respect your feelings but it will not add a point to your score.

7. Suggestions

   a. Objective-Type Questions

      (1) Examine the question booklet for proper sequence of pages and questions.

      (2) Read all instructions carefully.

      (3) Skip any question which seems too difficult; return to it after all other questions have been answered.

      (4) Apportion your time properly; do not spend too much time on any single question or group of questions.

      (5) Note and underline key words -- *all, most, fewest, least, best, worst, same, opposite.*

      (6) Pay particular attention to negatives.

      (7) Note unusual option, e.g., unduly long, short, complex, different or similar in content to the body of the question.

      (8) Observe the use of "hedging" words -- *probably, may, most likely, etc.*

      (9) Make sure that your answer is put next to the same number as the question.

      (10) Do not second-guess unless you have good reason to believe the second answer is definitely more correct.

      (11) Cross out original answer if you decide another answer is more accurate; do not erase.

      (12) Answer all questions; guess unless instructed otherwise.

      (13) Leave time for review.

   b. Essay-Type Questions

      (1) Read each question carefully.

      (2) Determine exactly what is wanted. Underline key words or phrases.

      (3) Decide on outline or paragraph answer.

      (4) Include many different points and elements unless asked to develop any one or two points or elements.

      (5) Show impartiality by giving pros and cons unless directed to select one side only.

      (6) Make and write down any assumptions you find necessary to answer the question.

      (7) Watch your English, grammar, punctuation, choice of words.

      (8) Time your answers; don't crowd material.

8. Answering the Essay Question

   Most essay questions can be answered by framing the specific response around several key words or ideas. Here are a few such key words or ideas:

M's: manpower, materials, methods, money, management;
P's: purpose, program, policy, plan, procedure, practice, problems, pitfalls, personnel, public relations.

a. <u>Six Basic Steps in Handling Problems</u>:

    (1) Preliminary plan and background development

    (2) Collect information, data and facts

    (3) Analyze and interpret information, data and facts

    (4) Analyze and develop solutions as well as make recommendations

    (5) Prepare report and sell recommendations

    (6) Install recommendations and follow up effectiveness

b. <u>Pitfalls to Avoid</u>

    (1) *Taking things for granted*

       A statement of the situation does not necessarily imply that each of the elements is necessarily true; for example, a complaint may be invalid and biased so that all that can be taken for granted is that a complaint has been registered.

    (2) *Considering only one side of a situation*

       Wherever possible, indicate several alternatives and then point out the reasons you selected the best one.

    (3) *Failing to indicate follow-up*

       Whenever your answer indicates action on your part, make certain that you will take proper follow-up action to see how successful your recommendations, procedures, or actions turn out to be.

    (4) *Taking too long in answering any single question*

       Remember to time your answers properly.

IX. AFTER THE TEST

Scoring procedures differ in detail among civil service jurisdictions although the general principles are the same. Whether the papers are hand-scored or graded by the electric scoring machine we have described, they are nearly always graded by number. That is, the person who marks the paper knows only the number -- never the name -- of the applicant. Not until all the papers have been graded will they be matched with names. If other tests, such as training and experience or oral interview ratings have been given, scores will be combined. Different parts of the examination usually have different weights. For example, the written test might count 60 percent of the final grade, and a rating of training and experience 40 percent. In many jurisdictions, veterans will have a certain number of points added to their grades.

After the final grade has been determined, the names are placed in grade order and an eligible list is established. There are various methods for resolving ties between those who get the same final grade: probably the most common is to place first the name of the person whose application was received first. Job offers are made from the eligible list in the order the names appear on it.

You will be notified of your grade and your rank order as soon as all these computations have been made. This will be done as rapidly as possible.

People who are found to meet the requirements in the announcement are called "eligibles." Their names are put on a list of eligibles. An eligible's chances of getting a job depend on how high he stands on this list and how fast agencies are filling jobs from the list.

When a job is to be filled from a list of eligibles, the agency asks for the names of people on the list of eligibles for that job.

When the civil service commission receives this request, it sends to the agency the names of the three people highest on the list. Or, if the job to be filled has specialized requirements, the office sends the agency, from the general list, the names of the top three persons who meet those requirements.

The appointing officer makes a choice from among the three people whose names were sent to him. If the selected person accepts the appointment, the names of the others are put back on the list to be considered for future openings.

That is the rule in hiring from all kinds of eligible lists, whether they are for typist, carpenter, chemist, or something else. For every vacancy, the appointing officer has his choice of any one of the top three eligibles on the list. This explains why the person whose name is on top of the list sometimes does not get an appointment when some of the persons lower on the list do. If the appointing officer chooses the No.2 or No.3 eligible, the No.1 eligible does not get a job at once, but stays on the list until he is appointed or the list is terminated.

X. HOW TO PASS THE INTERVIEW TEST

The examination for which you applied requires an oral interview test. You have already taken the written test and you are now being called for the interview test -- the final part of the formal examination.

You may think that it is not possible to prepare for an interview test and that there are no procedures to follow during an interview.

Our purpose is to point out some things you can do in advance that will help you and some good rules to follow and pitfalls to avoid while you are being interviewed.

A. *WHAT IS AN INTERVIEW SUPPOSED TO TEST?*

The written examination is designed to test the technical knowledge and competence of the candidate; the oral is designed to evaluate intangible qualities, not readily measured otherwise, and to establish a list showing the relative fitness of each candidate, *as measured against his competitors,* for the position sought. Scoring is not on the basis of "right" or "wrong," but on a sliding scale of values ranging from "not passable" to "outstanding." As a matter of fact, it is possible to achieve a relatively low score without a single "incorrect" answer because of evident weakness in the qualities being measured,

Occasionally, an examination may consist entirely of an oral test -- either an individual or a group oral. In such cases, information is sought concerning the technical knowledges and abilities of the candidate, since there has been no written examination for this purpose. More commonly, however, an oral test is used to supplement a written examination.

B. *WHO CONDUCTS INTERVIEWS?*

The composition of oral boards varies among different jurisdictions. In nearly all, a representative of the personnel department serves as chairman. One of the members of the board may be a representative of the department in which the candidate would work. In some cases, "outside experts" are used, and, frequently, a business man or some other representative of the general public is asked to serve. Labor and management or other special groups may be represented. The aim is to secure the services of experts in the appropriate field.

However the board is composed, it is a good idea (and not at all improper or unethical) to ascertain in advance of the interview who the members are and what groups they represent. When you are introduced to them, you will have some idea of their backgrounds and interests, and at least you will not stutter and stammer over their names.

C. *WHAT TO DO BEFORE THE INTERVIEW*

While knowledge about the board members is useful and takes some of the surprise element out of the interview, there is other preparation which is more substantive. It *is* possible to prepare for an oral -- in several ways:

1. Keep a Copy of Your Application and Review it Carefully Before the Interview

   This may be the only document before the oral board, and the starting point of the interview. Know what experience and education you have listed there, and the sequence and dates of it. Sometimes the board will ask *you* to review the highlights of your experience for them; you should not have to hem and haw doing it.

2. Study the Class Specification and the Examination Announcement

   Usually, the oral board has one or both of these to guide them. The qualities, characteristics, or knowledges required by the position sought are stated in these documents. They offer valuable clues as to the nature of the oral interview. For example, if the job involves supervisory responsibilities, the announcement will usually indicate that knowledge of modern supervisory methods and the qualifications of the candidate as a supervisor will be tested. If so, you can expect such questions, frequently in the form of a hypothetical situation which you are expected to solve. *Never* go into an oral without knowledge of the duties and responsibilities of the job you seek.

3. Think Through Each Qualification Required

   Try to visualize the kind of questions *you* would ask if you were a board member. How well could you answer them? Try especially to appraise your own knowledge and background in each area, *measured against the job sought*, and identify any areas in which you are weak. Be critical and realistic -- do not flatter yourself.

4. Do Some General Reading in Areas in Which You Feel You May be Weak

   For example, if the job involves supervision and your past experience has *not*, some general reading in supervisory methods and practices, particularly in the field of human relations, might be useful. *Do not* study agency procedures or detailed manuals. The oral board will be testing your understanding and capacity, *not* your memory.

5. Get a Good Night's Sleep and Watch Your General Health and Mental Attitude

   You will want a clear head at the interview. Take care of a cold or other minor ailment, and, of course, *no hangovers*.

D. WHAT TO DO THE DAY OF THE INTERVIEW

Now comes the day of the interview itself. Give yourself plenty of time to get there. Plan to arrive somewhat ahead of the scheduled time, particularly if your appointment is in the fore part of the day. If a previous candidate fails to appear, the board might be ready for you a bit early. By early afternoon an oral board is almost invariably behind schedule if there are many candidates, and you may have to wait. Take along a book or magazine to read, or your application to review. But leave any extraneous material in the waiting room when you go in for your interview. In any event, relax and compose yourself.

The matter of dress is important. The board is forming impressions about you -- from your experience, your manners, your attitudes, and from your appearance. Give your personal appearance careful attention. Dress your *best*, but not your flashiest. Choose conservative, appropriate clothing, and be sure it and you are immaculate. This is a business interview, and your appearance should indicate that you regard it as such. Besides, being well-groomed and properly dressed will help boost your confidence.

Sooner or later, someone will call your name and escort you into the interview room. *This is it.* From here on you are on your own. It is too late for any more preparation. But, remember, you asked for this opportunity to prove your fitness, and you are here because your request was granted.

E. WHAT HAPPENS WHEN YOU GO IN?

The usual sequence of events will be as follows: The clerk (who is often the board stenographer) will introduce you to the chairman of the oral board, who will introduce you to each other member of the board. Acknowledge the introductions before you sit down. Do not be surprised if you find a microphone facing you or a stenotypist sitting by. Oral interviews are usually recorded, in the event of an appeal or other review.

Usually the chairman of the board will open the interview by reviewing the highlights of your education and work experience from your application -- primarily for the benefit of the other members of the board, as well as to get the material into the record. Do not interrupt or comment unless there is an error or significant misinterpretation; if so, do not hesitate. But do not quibble about insignificant matters. Usually, also, he will ask you some question about your education, your experience, or your present job -- partly to get you started talking, to establish the interviewing "rapport." He may start the actual questioning, or turn it over to one of the other members. Frequently each member undertakes the questioning on a particular area, one in which he is perhaps most competent. So you can expect each member to participate in the examination. And because the time is limited, you may expect some rather abrupt switches in the direction the questioning takes. Do not be upset by it. Normally, a board member will not pursue a single line of questioning unless he discovers a particular strength or weakness.

After each member has participated, the chairman will usually ask whether any member has any further questions, then will ask you if you have anything you wish to add. Unless you are expecting this question, it may floor you. Or worse, it may start you off on an extended, extemporaneous speech. The board is not usually seeking more information. The question is principally to offer you a last opportunity to present further qualifications or to indicate that you have nothing to add. So, if you feel that a significant qualification or characteristic has been overlooked, it is proper to point it out in a sentence or so. Do not compliment the board on the thoroughness of their examination -- they have been sketchy, and you know it. If you wish, merely say, "No thank you, I have nothing further to add." This is a point where you can "talk yourself out" of a good impression or fail to present an important bit of information. *Remember, you close the interview yourself.*

The chairman will then say,"That is all,Mr.Smith,thank you." Do not be startled; the interview is over, and quicker than you think. Say,"Thank you and good morning," gather up your belongings and take your leave. Save your sigh of relief for the other side of the door.

F. HOW TO PUT YOUR BEST FOOT FORWARD

Throughout all this process, you may feel that the board individually and collectively is trying to pierce your defenses, to seek out your hidden weaknesses, and to embarrass and confuse you. Actually, this is not true. They are obliged to make an appraisal of your qualifications for the job you are seeking, and they *want to see you in your best light*. Remember, they must interview all candidates and a noncooperative candidate may become a failure in spite of their best efforts to bring out his qualifications. Here are fifteen(15) suggestions that will help you:

1. Be Natural. Keep Your Attitude Confident,But Not Cocky

If *you* are not confident that you can do the job, do not expect the *board* to be. Do not apologize for your weaknesses, try to bring out your strong points. The board is interested in a positive, not a negative presentation. Cockiness will antagonize any board member, and make him wonder if you are covering up a weakness by a false show of strength.

2. Get Comfortable, But Don't Lounge or Sprawl

Sit erectly but not stiffly. A careless posture may lead the board to conclude you are careless in other things, or at least that you are not impressed by the importance of the occasion to you.Either conclusion is natural, even if incorrect. Do not fuss with your clothing, or with a pencil or an ashtray. Your hands may occasionally be useful to emphasize a point; do not let them become a point of distraction.

3. Do Not Wisecrack or Make Small Talk

This is a serious situation, and your attitude should show that you consider it as such. Further, the time of the board is limited; they do not want to waste it, and neither should you.

4. Do Not Exaggerate Your Experience or Abilities

In the first place, from information in the application,from other interviews and other sources, the board may know more about you than you think; in the second place, you probably will not get away with it in the first place. An experienced board is rather adept at spotting such a situation. Do not take the chance.

5. If You Know a Member of the Board, Do Not Make a Point of It, Yet Do Not Hide It.

Certainly you are not fooling him, and probably not the other members of the board. Do not try to take advantage of your acquaintanceship -- it will probably do you little good.

6. Do Not Dominate the Interview

Let the board do that. They will give you the clues -- do not assume that you have to do all the talking. Realize that the board has a number of questions to ask you, and do not try to take up all the interview time by showing off your extensive knowledge of the answer to the first one.

7. <u>Be Attentive</u>

You only have twenty minutes or so, and you should keep your attention at its sharpest throughout. When a member is addressing a problem or a question to you, give him your undivided attention. Address your reply principally to him, but do not exclude the other members of the board.

8. <u>Do Not Interrupt</u>

A board member may be stating a problem for you to analyze. He will ask you a question when the time comes. Let him state the problem, and wait for the question.

9. <u>Make Sure You Understand the Question</u>

Do not try to answer until you are sure what the question is. If it is not clear, restate it in your own words or ask the board member to clarify it for you. But do not haggle about minor elements.

10. <u>Reply Promptly But Not Hastily</u>

A common entry on oral board rating sheets is "candidate responded readily," or "candidate hesitated in replies." Respond as promptly and quickly as you can, but do not jump to a hasty, ill-considered answer.

11. <u>Do Not Be Peremptory in Your Answers</u>

A brief answer is proper -- but do not fire your answer back. That is a losing game from your point of view. The board member can probably ask questions much faster than you can answer them.

12. <u>Do Not Try To Create the Answer You Think the Board Member Wants</u>

He is interested in what kind of ·· mind you have and how it works -- not in playing games. Furthermore, he can usually spot this practice and will usually grade you down on it.

13. <u>Do Not Switch Sides in Your Reply Merely to Agree With a Board Member</u>

Frequently, a member will take a contrary position merely to draw you out and to see if you are willing and able to defend your point of view. Do not start a debate, yet do not surrender a good position. If a position is worth taking, it is worth defending.

1 <u>Do Not Be Afraid to Admit an Error in Judgment if You Are Shown to Be Wrong</u>

The board knows that you are forced to reply without any opportunity for careful consideration. Your answer may be demonstrably wrong. If so, admit it and get on with the interview.

15. <u>Do Not Dwell at Length on Your Present Job</u>

The opening question may relate to your present assignment. Answer the question but do not go into an extended discussion. You are being examined for a *new* job, not your present one. As a matter of fact, try to phrase *all* your answers in terms of the job for which you are being examined.

G. BASIS OF RATING

Probably you will forget most of these "do's" and "don'ts" when you walk into the oral interview room. Even remembering them all will not insure you a passing grade. Perhaps you did not have the qualifications in the first place. But remembering them *will* help you to put your best foot forward, without treading on the toes of the board members.

Rumor and popular opinion to the contrary notwithstanding, an oral board wants you to make the best appearance possible. They know you are under pressure -- but they also want to see how you respond to it as a guide to what your reaction would be under the pressures of the job you seek. They will be influenced by the degree of poise you display, the personal traits you show, and the manner in which you respond.

EXAMINATION SECTION

EXAMINATION SECTION

TEST 1

DIRECTIONS: Each question or incomplete statement is followed by
several suggested answers or completions. Select the
one that BEST answers the question or completes the
statement. *PRINT THE LETTER OF THE CORRECT ANSWER IN
THE SPACE AT THE RIGHT.*

Questions 1-5.

DIRECTIONS: Questions 1 through 5 are to be answered SOLELY on the
basis of the information, contribution rate table, and
list of *physically-taxing* positions given below.

*A member's normal contributions to the retirement annuity fund
are made through payroll deductions. Various factors, including the
member's age on the date of enrollment in the system, the date of
enrollment in the system, and whether the type of work he performs
has been classified as "physically-taxing" or "non-physically-taxing,"
determine his rate of contribution. Such rate is then applied against
his gross earnings in order to determine his actual contribution.*

*A member's age is computed to his closest age; e.g., 24 years,
6 months = 25 years; 24 years 5 months, 29 days = 24 years. Thirty
(30) days is assumed to be equal to 1 month.*

*The table below represents, in a condensed form, contribution
rates for members of a retirement system according to age, date of
enrollment in the system, and whether the position is "physically-
taxing" or"non-physically-taxing." Following the table is a list of
selected positions which have been classified as "physically-taxing."*

CONTRIBUTION RATE TABLE

Age on Date of Enroll-ment	Yearly Rates for Non-Physically-Taxing Positions		Yearly Rates for Physically-Taxing Positions	
	Enrollment Prior to 1/1/84	Enrollment After 1/1/84	Enrollment Prior to 1/1/84	Enrollment After 1/1/84
18	7.55	8.15	8.35	9.00
19	7.20	7.80	7.95	8.60
20	6.90	7.45	7.65	8.25
21	6.65	7.20	7.35	7.90
22	6.45	6.95	7.10	7.65
23	6.25	6.75	6.95	7.45
24	6.10	6.60	6.75	7.30
25	6.00	6.50	6.65	7.15
26	5.90	6.40	6.40	6.90
27	5.80	6.30	6.20	6.70
28	5.75	6.20	6.00	6.45
29	5.65	6.15	5.80	6.25
30	5.60	6.05	5.60	6.05
31	5.40	5.85	5.40	5.85
32	5.25	5.65	5.25	5.65
33	5.05	5.50	5.05	5.50
34	4.90	5.30	4.90	5.30
35	4.75	5.15	4.75	5.15

List of Selected *Physically-Taxing* Positions

Able Seaman	Deckhand	Handyman
Asphalt Worker	Deputy Sheriff	Laborer
Auto Machinist	Electrician	Plumber
Auto Mechanic	Elevator Mechanic	Sign Painter
Bricklayer	Exterminator	Stockman
Cement Mason	Gardener	Welder
Climber and Pruner	Glazier	Window Cleaner

1. An employee who enrolled in the system at age 26 in 1985 as an Elevator Operator pays a pension rate of
   A. 5.90%   B. 6.40%   C. 6.90%   D. 7.15

2. A Motorman earning $16,000 per annum who enrolled in the system in 1991 at age 34 has pension deductions which total, on an annual basis,
   A. $784.00   B. $808.00   C. $848.00   D. $880.00

3. If a Gardener's salary is $235.00 per week and he enrolled in the system at age 21 in 2002, his contribution for the year is MOST NEARLY
   A. $879.84   B. $898.17   C. $934.83   D. $965.38

4. A Statistician who earns a bi-weekly salary of $295.00, who enrolled in the system on October 12, 2002, and whose date of birth is February 15, 1971, makes a bi-weekly pension contribution in the amount of
   A. $15.49   B. $16.22   C. $16.67   D. $17.27

5. A Stockman who enrolled in the system on August 6, 2000, whose date of birth is April 25, 1976 and who earns $183.00 per week, makes an annual pension contribution of MOST NEARLY
   A. $628.06   B. $642.33   C. $694.67   D. $708.94

Questions 6-10.

DIRECTIONS: Questions 6 through 10 are to be answered SOLELY on the basis of the information and the chart which follow.

Advance payment checks are issued to retirees prior to final determination of the actual retirement allowance. The formula for computing monthly advance payments varies with the pension plan.

MONTHLY ADVANCE PAYMENT FORMULA		
Plan A	Plan B	Service Fraction Plan
1/12 x 44% of last posted calendar year's earnings	1/12 x number of years of service x 1.2% of last posted calendar year's earnings	1% of total accumulated salary deductions

6. A retiree whose last year's earnings were $18,276 and who was eligible to retire under Plan A will receive monthly advance payments of MOST NEARLY
    A. $182.76   B. $402.07   C. $670.12   D. $804.14   6.____

7. A member of Plan A who retired at a salary of $9,898 after 12 years of service will receive monthly advance payments in the amount of MOST NEARLY
    A. $98.98   B. $118.77   C. $362.92   D. $435.51   7.____

8. Six months of advance payments for a member of a Service Fraction Plan whose accumulated salary deductions totalled $8,300 amount to
    A. $83.00   B. $498.00   C. $597.60   D. $830.00   8.____

9. A member of Plan A received advance checks for three months totalling $1,425.82.
The salary on which his advance payments were based was MOST NEARLY
    A. $11,592   B. $12,962   C. $13,042   D. $13,562   9.____

10. Suppose that an employee's membership date was 12/31/78, his retirement date was 12/31/97, and his last year's salary was $14,230.
What is his monthly advance payment under Plan B?
    A. $170.37   B. $238.66   C. $270.37   D. $284.60   10.____

Question 11.

DIRECTIONS: Answer Question 11 SOLELY on the basis of the information in the paragraph below.

Final compensation shall mean the average annual compensation earnable by a member for city service during his last five years of city service, or during any other five consecutive years of member or restored member service which such member shall designate.

11. According to the information contained in the above statement, a member who worked for the city from January 1, 1960 to December 31, 1997 could designate, for purposes of determining his final compensation, the years
    A. 1/1/92 to 12/31/97
    B. 1/1/90 to 12/31/94 and 1/1/93 to 12/31/97
    C. 1/1/91 to 12/31/95
    D. 1/1/90 to 12/31/92 and 1/1/94 to 12/31/95   11.____

Questions 12-15.

DIRECTIONS: Questions 12 through 15 are to be answered SOLELY on the basis of the information in the passage below.

An employee who has been a member of the retirement system continuously for at least two years may thereafter borrow an amount not exceeding forty percent of the amount of his accumulated contributions in the retirement system, provided that he can repay the amount borrowed, with interest, before he reaches age sixty-three by additional deductions of eight percent from his compensation at the time it is paid. The rate of interest payable on such loan shall be three percent higher than the rate of regular interest creditable to his retirement account. The amount borrowed, with interest, shall be repaid in equal installments by deduction from the member's compensation at the time it is paid, but such installments must be equal to at least four percent of the member's compensation.

Each loan shall be insured by the retirement system against the death of the member, as follows: from the twenty-fifth through the fiftieth day after making the loan, thirty percent of the present value of the loan is insured; from the fifty-first through the seventy-fifth day, sixty percent of the present value of the loan is insured; on and after the seventy-sixth day, all of the present value of the loan is insured. Upon the death of the member, the amount of insurance payable shall be credited to his accumulated contributions to the retirement system.

Instead of a loan, any member who cancels his rate of contribution may withdraw from his account, and may restore in any year he chooses, any sum in excess of the maximum in his annuity savings account and due to his account at the end of the calendar year in which he was entitled to cancel his rate of contribution.

12. Based on the information in the above passage, a member   12.___
     may obtain a loan
     A. in any amount not exceeding forty percent of his
         accumulated contributions in the system
     B. if he has contributions in excess of the maximum
         in his annuity savings account
     C. if he will remain a member of the retirement system
         until age 63
     D. once during his first two years of membership and
         then at any time thereafter

13. According to the information in the above passage, the   13.___
     interest rate paid by a member who borrows from the
     retirement system is
     A. 4% of his earnable compensation
     B. 8% of his earnable compensation
     C. lower than the interest rate creditable to his
         retirement account
     D. higher than the interest rate creditable to his
         retirement account

14. Suppose that a member of the retirement system obtained a   14.___
     loan on July 15 of this year and died on October 2 when
     the present value of her loan was $800.
     Based on the information in the above passage, this member
     will have ____ her accumulated contributions to the retire-
     ment system.
         A. $480 credited to   B. $480 deducted from
         C. $800 credited to   D. $800 deducted from

15. Based on the information in the above passage, a member   15.___
who has excess funds in his retirement account may with-
draw funds from the retirement system
A. if he has cancelled his rate of contribution
B. if he restores the funds within one year of withdrawal
C. when he retires
D. if he leaves city service

Questions 16-20.

DIRECTIONS: Questions 16 through 20 are to be answered SOLELY on
the basis of the information in the passage below.

*Upon the death of a member or former member of the retirement
system, there shall be paid to his estate, or to the person he had
nominated by written designation, his accumulated deductions. In
addition, if he is a member who is in city service, there shall be
paid a sum consisting of: an amount equal to the compensation he
earned while a member during the three months immediately preceding
his death, or, if the total amount of years of allowable service
exceeds five, there shall be paid an amount equal to the compensation
he earned while a member during the six months immediately preceding
his death; and the reserve-for-increased-take-home-pay, if any.
Payment for the expense of burial, not exceeding two hundred and
fifty dollars, may be made to the relative or friend who, in the
absence or failure of the designated beneficiary, assumes this
responsibility.*

*Until the first retirement benefit payment has been made, where
a member has not selected an option, the member will be considered
to be in city service, and the death benefits provided above will be
paid instead of the retirement allowance. The member, or upon his
death his designated beneficiary, may provide that the actuarial
equivalent of the benefit otherwise payable in a lump sum shall be
paid in the form of an annuity payable in installments; the amount
of such annuity is determined at the time of the member's death on
the basis of the age of the beneficiary at that time.*

16. Suppose that a member who has applied for retirement   16.___
benefits without selecting an option dies before receiving
any payments.
According to the information in the above passage, this
member's beneficiary would be entitled to receive
A. an annuity based on the member's age at the time of
his death
B. a death benefit only
C. the member's retirement allowance only
D. the member's retirement allowance, plus a death
benefit payment in a lump sum

17. Suppose that a member died on June 15, 1997, while still   17.___
in city service. He had joined the retirement system in
March, 1980. During the year preceding his death, he
earned $37,500.
Based on the information in the above passage, the designated
beneficiary of this member would be entitled to receive all
of the following EXCEPT

A. a payment of $18,750
B. payment of burial expense up to $750
C. the member's accumulated deductions
D. the reserve-for-increased-take-home-pay, if any

18. According to the information in the above passage, the   18.____
amount of the benefit payable upon the death of a member
is based, in part, on the
A. length of city service during which the deceased
person was a member
B. number of beneficiaries the deceased member had
nominated
C. percent of the deceased member's deductions for
social security
D. type of retirement plan to which the deceased member
belonged

19. According to the information in the above passage, which   19.____
one of the following statements concerning the payment of
death benefits is CORRECT?
A. In order for a death benefit to be paid, the deceased
member must have previously nominated, in writing,
someone to receive the benefit.
B. Death benefits are paid upon the death of members who
are in city service.
C. A death benefit must be paid in one lump sum.
D. When a retired person dies, his retirement allowance
is replaced by a death benefit payment.

20. According to the information in the above passage, the   20.____
amount of annuity payments made to a beneficiary in monthly
installments in lieu of a lump-sum payment is determined
by the
A. length of member's service at the time of his death
B. age of the beneficiary at the time of the member's
death
C. member's age at retirement
D. member's age at the time of his death

KEY (CORRECT ANSWERS)

1.	B	11.	C
2.	C	12.	A
3.	D	13.	D
4.	C	14.	C
5.	C	15.	A
6.	C	16.	B
7.	C	17.	B
8.	B	18.	A
9.	B	19.	B
10.	C	20.	B

TEST 2

DIRECTIONS: Each question or incomplete statement is followed by several suggested answers or completions. Select the one that BEST answers the question or completes the statement. *PRINT THE LETTER OF THE CORRECT ANSWER IN THE SPACE AT THE RIGHT.*

Questions 1-8.

DIRECTIONS: Questions 1 through 8 are to be answered SOLELY on the basis of the information contained in the passage and the *Work History* given below.

The pension benefit a retiree receives is determined by the number of years the employee worked for the city while a member of the retirement system (service credit) and the wages earned during specific periods of time (compensation).

Following are some rules regarding the computation of service credit:

• Service credit accrues from the date the employee becomes a member of the retirement system through the last day he works.

• Service credit is computed separately for each calendar year.

• Six days of service credit, called "forgiveness," is given for each month actually worked in a calendar year, except in the employee's first year of service, where he is limited to service credit not exceeding the time between the date of membership and the end of said calendar year, and in his last year of service, where he is limited to service credit not exceeding the time between the beginning of the last year and the date of retirement.

• A member receives full service credit for periods of military service. He also receives credit for military service for the period between discharge from military service and return to city service, provided he returned to work within 90 days of his discharge.

• A member who is on leave of absence for an entire calendar year does not receive any service credit for that year.

• A member may NOT earn more than one year of service credit in a calendar year.

NOTE: For the purpose of answering Questions 1 through 8, assume that 30 days = 1 month, and that a calendar year is January 1 to December 31.

Work History of Employee X

January 1, 1968	Entered city service
July 1, 1968	Became a member of retirement system
September 15, 1969	Began leave of absence
September 30, 1969	Returned from leave of absence
July 1, 1971	Entered military service
January 31, 1973	Discharged from military service
March 10, 1973	Returned to city service
June 1, 1982	Began leave of absence
August 31, 1984	Returned from leave of absence
October 31, 1996	Last day worked
November 1, 1996	Retired

1. How much service credit did the member earn in 1968?   1.___
   A. 6 months   B. 6 months and 6 days
   C. 7 months and 12 days   D. 1 year

2. How much service credit did the member earn in 1969?   2.___
   A. 9 months   B. 11 months
   C. 11 months and 6 days   D. 1 year

3. How much service credit did the member earn in 1971?   3.___
   A. 6 months   B. 7 months
   C. 7 months and 42 days   D. 12 months

4. How much service credit did the member earn in 1984?   4.___
   A. 4 months   B. 4 months and 3 days
   C. 4 months and 24 days   D. 6 months

5. How much service credit did the member earn in 1996?   5.___
   A. 2 months   B. 10 months
   C. 10 months and 1 day   D. 1 year

6. The member earned LESS than 4 months of service credit in   6.___
   the year

   A. 1972   B. 1982   C. 1983   D. 1984

7. What is the total of the service credit which the member   7.___
   was given for his military service?
   A. 1 year and 7 months
   B. 1 year, 8 months, and 10 days
   C. 1 year, 9 months, and 10 days
   D. 1 year, 10 months, and 10 days

8. What is the TOTAL amount of days of *forgiveness* which was   8.___
   granted to the member?
   A. 54   B. 69   C. 90   D. 96

Questions 9-12.

DIRECTIONS: Questions 9 through 12 are to be answered SOLELY on
the basis of the information in the passage below.

*Any member of the retirement system who is in city service, who
files a proper application for service credit and agrees to deductions
from his compensation at triple his normal rate of contribution, shall
be credited with a period of city service previous to the beginning of
his present membership in the retirement system. The period of service
credited shall be equal to the period throughout which such triple
deductions are made, but may not exceed the total of the city service
the member rendered between his first day of eligibility for membership in the retirement system and the day he last became a member.
After triple contributions for all of the first three years of service
credit claimed, the remaining service credit may be purchased by a
single payment of the sum of the remaining payments. If the total
time purchasable exceeds ten years, triple contributions may be made
for one-half of such time, and the remaining time purchased by a
single payment of the sum of the remaining payments. Credit for
service acquired in the above manner may be used only in determining
the amount of any retirement benefit. Eligibility for such benefit
will in all cases be based upon service rendered after the employee's
membership last began, and will be exclusive of service credit purchased as described above.*

9.   According to the above passage, in order to obtain credit   9.___
      for city service previous to the beginning of an employee's
      present membership in the retirement system, the employee
      must
          A. apply for the service credit and consent to additional
             contributions to the retirement system
          B. apply for the service credit before he renews his
             membership in the retirement system
          C. have previous city service which does not exceed ten
             years
          D. make contributions to the retirement system for
             three years

10.   According to the information in the above passage, credit   10.___
      for city service previous to the beginning of an employee's
      present membership in the retirement system is
          A. credited up to a maximum of ten years
          B. credited up to any member of the retirement system
          C. used in determining the amount of the employee's
             benefits
          D. used in establishing the employee's eligibility to
             receive benefits

11.   According to the information in the above passage, a   11.___
      member of the retirement system may purchase service
      credit for
          A. the period of time between his first day of eligibility
             for membership in the retirement system and the date
             he applies for the service credit

    B. one-half of the total of his previous city service
       if the total time exceeds ten years
    C. the period of time throughout which triple deductions
       are made
    D. the period of city service between his first day of
       eligibility for membership in the retirement system
       and the day he last became a member

12. Suppose that a member of the retirement system has filed   12.___
an application for service credit for five years of previous
city service.
Based on the information in the above passage, the employee
may purchase credit for this previous city service by making
    A. triple contributions for three years
    B. triple contributions for one-half of the time and a
       single payment of the sum of the remaining payments
    C. triple contributions for three years and a single
       payment of the sum of the remaining payments
    D. a single payment of the sum of the payments

Questions 13-20.

DIRECTIONS: Questions 13 through 20 consist of lines of names, dates,
and numbers which represent the names, membership dates,
social security numbers, and membership numbers of
members of the retirement system.

For each question, you are to choose the option (A, B,
C, or D) which exactly matches the information appearing
next to the question number.

SAMPLE QUESTION

Crossen   12/23/91   173568929   253492
    A. Crossen 2/23/91   173568929   253492
    B. Crossen 12/23/91   173568729   253492
    C. Crossen 12/23/91   173568929   253492
    D. Crossan 12/23/91   173568929   258492

The correct answer is C. Only Option C shows the name,
date, and numbers exactly as they are shown next to the
question number. Option A has a mistake in the date.
Option B has a mistake in the social security number.
Option D has a mistake in the name and in the membership
number.

13. Figueroa   1/15/99   119295386   147563   13.___
    A. Figueroa   1/5/99   119295386   147563
    B. Figueroa   1/15/99   119295386   147563
    C. Figueroa   1/15/99   119295836   147563
    D. Figueroa   1/15/99   119295886   147563

14. Goodridge   6/19/94   106237869   128352   14.___
    A. Goodridge   6/19/94   106287869   128332
    B. Goodrigde   6/19/94   106237869   128352
    C. Goodridge   6/9/94   106237869   128352
    D. Goodridge   6/19/94   106237869   128352

15. Balsam   9/13/92   109652382   116938   15.____
    A. Balsan   9/13/92   109652382   116938
    B. Balsam   9/13/92   109652382   116938
    C. Balsom   9/13/92   109652382   116938
    D. Balsalm 9/13/92   109652382   116938

16. Mackenzie 2/16/84   127362513   101917   16.____
    A. Makenzie 2/16/84   127362513   101917
    B. Mackenzie 2/16/84   127362513   101917
    C. Mackenzie 2/16/84   127362513   101977
    D. Mackenzie 2/16/84   127862513   101917

17. Halpern   12/2/88   115206359   286070   17.____
    A. Halpern   12/2/88   115206359   286070
    B. Halpern   12/2/88   113206359   286070
    C. Halpern   12/2/88   115206359   206870
    D. Halpern   12/2/88   115206359   286870

18. Phillips   4/8/81   137125516   192612   18.____
    A. Phillips   4/8/81   137125516   196212
    B. Philipps   4/8/81   137125516   192612
    C. Phillips   4/8/81   137125516   192612
    D. Phillips   4/8/81   137122516   192612

19. Francisce 11/9/78   123926037   152210   19.____
    A. Francisce 11/9/78   123826837   152210
    B. Francisce 11/9/78   123926037   152210
    C. Francisce 11/9/78   123936037   152210
    D. Franscice 11/9/78   123926037   152210

20. Silbert   7/28/89   118421999   178514   20.____
    A. Silbert   7/28/89   118421999   178544
    B. Silbert   7/28/89   184421999   178514
    C. Silbert   7/28/89   118421999   178514
    D. Siblert   7/28/89   118421999   178514

KEY (CORRECT ANSWERS)

1. A	11. D
2. D	12. C
3. D	13. B
4. C	14. D
5. B	15. B
6. C	16. B
7. B	17. A
8. B	18. C
9. A	19. B
10. C	20. C

EXAMINATION SECTION
TEST 1

DIRECTIONS:
    Each question or incomplete statement is followed by several sug-
gested answers or completions. Select the one that *BEST* answers the
question or completes the statement. *PRINT THE LETTER OF THE CORRECT
ANSWER IN THE SPACE AT THE RIGHT.*

1. You are interviewing a patient who is evasive and unre-   1. ...
   sponsive to your questions. When you ask about his
   hospital coverage, he tells you about his life insurance.
   In order to obtain specific answers from this patient,
   of the following, your *MOST* effective approach would be to
      A. allow the patient to ramble, since he will eventually
         answer your questions
      B. ask direct, pointed questions which require short,
         simple answers
      C. tell him that if he does not answer your questions,
         he will have to pay the bill himself
      D. ask a nurse to be present during the interview as
         a witness to the patient's refusal to cooperate

2. An insurance carrier calls you to request information   2. ...
   from a medical record for a patient who has made application for life insurance. Generally, the *proper*
   way for you to handle this request would be to
      A. give the carrier the information, since the patient
         cannot obtain life insurance until the medical in-
         formation is released
      B. advise the carrier that you cannot give out any
         medical information whatever
      C. advise the carrier that the information is privileged
         and confidential, and can be released only with the
         patient's authorization
      D. send a copy of the medical record to the patient and
         have him forward it to the carrier so he can obtain
         his life insurance

3. All of the following statements are in accord with the   3. ...
   goals or benefits of the Medicaid program *EXCEPT:*
      A. Medicaid eligibles have the right to avail themselves
         of the services of any institution, agency or person
         qualified to participate in the Medicaid program
      B. High-quality medical care will be made available to
         everyone regardless of race, age, national origin or
         economic standing
      C. Hospitals must provide the same standard of medical
         care and health services to Medicaid eligibles as to
         any self-paying patient
      D. Medicaid benefits will be terminated when the cost
         of the patient's care exceeds a predetermined amount

4. As an investigator, you may be required to provide con-   4. ...
   crete services for some patients, when necessary. According to accepted terminology, *which one* of the following would be an example of a concrete service?

      A. Assuring a patient that "everything will be all right"
      B. Referring a patient to the department of social services for emergency assistance
      C. Obtaining a special favor for a patient such as a between-meal snack
      D. Moving a patient to a more pleasant ward in another part of the hospital

5. *Which one* of the following statements represents a *BASIC* similarity between Medicare and Medicaid?   5. ...
      A. Persons over 65 can qualify under both programs
      B. Both have the same minimum income requirements
      C. Both require a means test for determining eligibility
      D. Both have the same residency requirements

6. Of the following, the usual manner of payment for an eligible Medicaid patient utilizing health and hospitals services is from the   6. ...
      A. government to the patient
      B. government to the hospital
      C. government to the attending physician
      D. patient to the hospital

7. *Which one* of the following groups is *AUTOMATICALLY* eligible for Medicaid, according to Federal requirements?   7. ...
      A. Medically indigent persons, regardless of eligibility under any other public assistance program
      B. Medically indigent children under 21, regardless of the family's eligibility for categorical assistance
      C. Persons receiving all or part of their basic living expenses from public assistance
      D. Medically indigent persons who meet all but the income requirements for categorical assistance

8. The agency responsible for administration of payment for hospital services under the Medicaid program is the   8. ...
      A. City Department of Social Services
      B. City Department of Health
      C. City Health and Hospitals Corporation
      D. U. S. Department of Health, Education and Welfare

9. Of the following, a *distinction* between the Medicaid and Medicare programs is in the   9. ...
      A. clientele services   B. source of funding
      C. authorizing legislation
      D. types of services reimbursed

10. The *one* of the following health plans which is *NOT* paid for by the patient or a group is   10. ...
      A. Medicare   B. Blue Cross
      C. Medicaid   D. Health Insurance Plan

Questions 11-13.

DIRECTIONS: Answer Questions 11 through 13 based *SOLELY* on the following passage.

    In the field of investigation, the terms "interview" and "interrogation" have different meanings. The interview is an informal questioning for the purpose of learning facts. The objective of the interrogation is to obtain an admission of guilt, preferably in the form of a signed statement.

Successful interviewing requires that the investigator be able to learn, through questioning, what the person being interviewed has learned, or has observed through his sight, hearing, taste, smell, and touch. In order to gain the most benefit from an interview, the investigator must provide himself with a background of information before arranging the interview. Random questioning is seldom successful, and the investigator should be prepared to conduct the interview in a logical manner. Before opening an interview, the investigator must estimate what the interviewed person knows, or should know, about the subject of the investigation.

The investigator must always keep in mind that he has no power to force persons to give him information, and that he must often encourage the interviewee to cooperate. Many persons are unwilling to become involved, believing that any statement they give may involve them in future obligations. Obtaining a statement requires an acquaintance with psychological methods. Often an appeal to a person's sympathies will overcome his reluctance to become "involved."

11. According to the above passage, all of the following   11. ...
    techniques should be employed by an investigator *EXCEPT*
        A. gaining a preliminary estimate of an interviewee's knowledge of the subject under investigation
        B. appealing to an interviewee's sympathies
        C. utilizing random questioning
        D. utilizing background information

12. According to the passage, the *MAIN* difference between an   12. ...
    interrogation and an interview lies in the
        A. method by which information is obtained
        B. use to which the information is put
        C. type of person asking the questions
        D. background information needed before questioning begins

13. According to the passage, the interviewer should have a   13. ...
    knowledge of psychological methods in order to
        A. obtain an admission of guilt
        B. force the interviewee to cooperate
        C. encourage persons to become involved
        D. make the person sympathetic to the interviewer

Questions 14-16.

DIRECTIONS: Questions 14 through 16 are to be answered *SOLELY* on the gasis of the following passage.

An important question which arises from the concept of the right to a minimum standard of health care for all persons concerns the viability of the means test, which is a part of the Medicaid program. If the financial barrier is to be removed for the medically indigent, it is necessary to define who the medically indigent are. Paradoxically, the means test necessary to define the medically indigent may itself prove to be a significant barrier to adequate health care. The attitude of the poor towards the means test may prvent their using available services. If this proves to be true, the government must remove the barrier if it is to protect the right of the individual to health care. This does not, however, automatically require removing the means test. The government would be faced with a choice: remove the means test or change the attitude of the people toward the test. In devising Medicare, a means test was considered to be degrading; there was to be nothing second-class about the elderly. Rather than trying to change the idea that a means test is degrading, all people beyond a certain age were made eligible.

14. The *MOST* appropriate of the following titles for this   14. ...
    passage would be
    A. THE CONCEPT OF THE MEANS TEST IN MEDICAID AND MEDICARE
    B. HOW THE POOR VIEW THE MEANS TEST
    C. VIEWS ON HEALTH CARE FOR THE POOR
    D. THE MEANS TEST AS VIEWED BY THE ELDERLY

15. According to an implication made in the passage, in order 15. ...
    for the poor to derive maximum benefit from the Medicaid
    program, *which one* of the following conditions must be met?
    A. The means test must automatically be removed
    B. All persons, young and elderly, should be made eligible
    C. Public feeling about the means test should be changed
    D. The requirements for Medicaid should be similar to
       those of Medicare

16. The paradox alluded to in the passage refers to the   16. ...
    A. reluctance of the poor to use Medicaid, which was
       developed as a means of providing health care for the
       poor
    B. attitudes of the elderly, who considered the means
       test to be degrading, and, therefore, did not use
       Medicare
    C. difficulty of administering the means test, which is
       a necessary component of any program to define the
       medically indigent
    D. the government's decision to remove the means test
       as a Medicare requirement instead of changing the
       attitude of the elderly toward the test

Questions 17-20.

DIRECTIONS: Answer Questions 17 through 20 *SOLELY* on the basis of
the information contained in the following passage.

    The Aid to the Blind program calls for determination of blind-
ness and need, but in most other respects the statutory requirements
for the state plan are similar to those for Old Age Assistance (OAA).
Blindness need not be total to be considered qualifying for assistance.
The usual test of whether a person is deemed to be blind relates to the
ability to earn a livelihood, what is sometimes termed "economic
blindness." Need is ascertained by determining whether there is a
budget deficiency, as in OAA, except that the state may, in computing
need, disregard the first $85 per month of earned income, plus one-
half of earned income in excess of $85 per month; these sums are to
be taken into account after $5 of any income. With respect to age,
some states have no age limit, while others set 16, 18 or 21 years
at the lower limit, and some set the upper age limit as under 65 years.
It should be noted that, although some persons may meet the eligibility
specifications of more than one category, it is possible to receive a
monthly grant from only one of them. It is expected that every effort
will be made to enable blind persons to become self-supporting in some
measure. These include efforts by the recipients to cash grants to
move from dependency to independency, as well as referrals to social
service agencies in order to offer and facilitate rehabilitation opportunities.

17. As used in the above passage, the expression "economic   17. ...
    blindness" refers to a blind person's
       A. budget deficiency   B. capacity for self-support
       C. efforts toward rehabilitation
       D. eligibility specifications

4

18. According to the above passage, in computing the need   18. ...
    for assistance, *which one* of the following amounts is
    DISREGARDED for a blind person earning $200 per month?
       A. $122.50   B. $127.50   C. $132.50   D. $147.50
19. The *one* of the following criteria which is *NOT* mentioned 19. ...
    in the passage as a consideration in determining elibility
    for aid is
       A. age   B. financial need
       C. degree of blindness   D. education
20. On the basis of the above passage, it can be concluded   20. ...
    that an *important* aspect of the Aid to the Blind Program
    is to
       A. assist blind persons until they can achieve some
          degree of economic self-sufficiency
       B. encourage blind persons to establish their right to
          financial assistance
       C. provide direct social service and rehabilitation
          assistance to blind persons
       D. establish categories of assistance on the basis of
          degree of blindness

KEY (CORRECT ANSWERS)

1.	B	11.	C
2.	C	12.	B
3.	D	13.	C
4.	B	14.	A
5.	A	15.	C
6.	B	16.	A
7.	C	17.	B
8.	A	18.	D
9.	B	19.	D
10.	C	20.	A

TEST 2

DIRECTIONS:

Each question or incomplete statement is followed by several suggested answers or completions. Select the one that *BEST* answers the question or completes the statement. *PRINT THE LETTER OF THE CORRECT ANSWER IN THE SPACE AT THE RIGHT.*

Questions 1-4.

DIRECTIONS: Answer Questions 1 through 4 based *SOLELY* on the information on the Hospital Care Authorization and Claim Form given below.

Paul Forand was born on January 12, 1911 in Miami, Florida. His Medicare number is 064-26-3000A. At the time of his admission to Bell View Hospital, 100 First Ave., Manhattan, he was living with his wife, Mary Forand, and daughter, Debbie Forand, at 200 Second Avenue, Manhattan. He was admitted on April 10, 1985. The attending physician was John Smith. This was the second time he had ever been hospitalized. He was previously hospitalized on April 21, 1981 in Lexington Hill Hospital for a gall bladder operation.

On April 12, 1985 it was decided to transfer Paul Forand to Bleakman Midtown Hospital, 102 E. 29th Street, Manhattan, because his primary admitting diagnosis could be treated better at this facility. His attending physician at Bleakman Midtown Hospital was Richard Jones. On April 14, 1985, Mary Forand was informed that her husband would be discharged from the hospital at 4 p.m. that afternoon. She planned to leave early from her job as Securities Analyst with the firm of Farrell Winch to take her husband home.

Mary Forand is the head of the household. Her social security number is 624-60-0030.

HOSPITAL CARE AUTHORIZATION and CLAIM

DATE SUBMITTED	HOSPITAL NAME: Bell View Hospital	☐ OUT OF STATE HOSPITAL	HOSPITAL NO.	HOSPITAL ADMITTING NO.
PATIENT'S NAME: LAST / FIRST	AGE / RACE / SEX	BIRTH DATE	CATEGORY	MEDICAID NO. / SUFFIX / CENTER
PATIENT'S ADDRESS: NO. & STREET		TELEPHONE NO.	NAME ON MEDICAID CARD, OR HEAD OF HOUSEHOLD	
CITY (BOROUGH) 13	STATE	ZIP CODE 14	EXPIRATION DATE MO. YR. 26	D.S.S. 515A ☐ ATTACHED 27 / DATE ORIGINAL SUBMITTED ☐
PATIENT'S RELATIONSHIP TO HEAD OF HOUSEHOLD ☐ SELF ☐ SPOUSE ☐ DAUGHTER ☐ SON ☐ OTHER: 15			PREFIX / MEDICARE NO. / SUFFIX 28	
RESPONSIBLE PHYSICIAN FULL NAME 16		SOCIAL SECURITY NUMBER 17	NAME ON CUBAN REFUGEE CARD / CUBAN REFUGEE NO. 29	
PREVIOUS CARE - HOSPITAL NAME 18	NAME OF FAMILY MEMBER 19	DATE ADMITTED 20 / DATE DISCHARGED 21	WORKMAN'S COMP. ☐ YES ☐ NO 30	DISABILITY FORM ATTACHED ☐ AWARD LETTER ☐ D.S.S. 486 ☐ D.S.S. 115 31
DATE ADMITTED 32	HOUR A.M. P.M. 33	PRIMARY ADMITTING DIAGNOSIS 34 / CODE 35 / ACCOM. 36	TYPE OF ADMISSION ☐ ELECT. ☐ E R ☐ O B S ☐ ACUTE TRANS ☐ OTHER TRANS 37	
DATE FIRST SURGERY 38	FIRST MAJOR SURGERY 39	CODE 40	SECONDARY DISCHARGE DIAGNOSIS 45	CODE 46
DATE DISCHARGED 41	HOUR A.M. P.M. 42	PRIMARY DISCHARGE DIAGNOSIS 43 / CODE 44	TERTIARY DISCHARGE DIAGNOSIS 47	CODE 48
STATUS CIRCLE ONE 49	DISCHARGED 1 / STILL IN 2 / DIED 3 / TRANSFERRED TO 4	SPECIAL PROGRAM IF APPLICABLE CIRCLE ONE 50	PHC 1 / PREM 2 / NARC 3 / SFP 4 / T.B. INEL 5 / DIAL. PT B 6 / FAM PLAN 7 / S.C. 8	IND REF 9
TYPE OF CARE CIRCLE ONE 51	MED. SURG. A / MATERNITY B / ABORTION C / NEW BORN D / BOARDER BABY E / PSYCH FULL TIME F / PSYCH DAY G / CHRONIC J	PHIC K / ECF L	T.B. M / ALC. REH N / DIALYSIS P / RET. REH R	SPC
PATIENT STATES ACCIDENT CASE 52 ☐ YES ☐ NO	DATE OF INJURY 53 / HOUR A.M. P.M. 54	HOW INJURY SUSTAINED 55	POLICE SHIELD NO. 56	PRECINCT 57
	NAME, ADDRESS, LICENSE NO. ETC. OF PERSON ALLEGEDLY AT FAULT 58			

1. *Which* box should be checked in the space on the Hospital   1. ...
   Care Authorization and Claim Form labeled "Patient's
   Relationship to Head of Household?"
       A. Daughter   B. Self   C. Spouse   D. Other
2. *Which* box should be circled in the space on the Hospital   2. ...
   Care Authorization and Claim Form labeled "Status Circle
   One?"
       A. 1   B. 2   C. 3   D. 4
3. *Which one* of the following spaces on the Hospital Care   3. ...
   Authorization and Claim Form can *NOT* be completed based
   solely on the information given above?
       A. Medicare No.   B. Patient's Address
       C. Responsible Physician   D. Primary Admitting Diagnosis
4. *Which one* of the following dates should be entered in   4. ...
   the box labeled "Date Admitted" (box 20) on the Hospital
   Care Authorization and Claim Form?
       A. April 21, 1981   B. April 10, 1985
       C. April 12, 1985   D. April 14, 1985

Questions 5-8.
DIRECTIONS: Answer Questions 5 through 8 *SOLELY* on the basis of
the information obtained in the patient interview and from the
previous admission record given below.

PATIENT INTERVIEW

     As a Hospital Care Investigator, you have interviewed a patient,
Giselle Krebs, who was admitted to the hospital with a fractured hip
on March 12, 1985, by her physician, Jane Kelly. The patient has
told you that she resides at 2801 Roger Avenue, Brooklyn, N. Y.,
with her retired husband, Sandor, and their daughter and son-in-law.
Her next of kin is her eldest daughter, Julie Cohen, who resides at
5025 Van Buren Street, Miami, Florida. Mrs. Krebs is employed by
Green View Gardens, 2802 Holbrook Boulevard, Brooklyn, New York, as
a part-time saleslady and has been in their employ for 3 years.
Her only health insurance coverage is that provided by Green Cross/
Green Shield, certificate number 707-36-5491.

     At the end of the interview Mrs. Krebs tells you that she had
previously been admitted to this hospital on July 12, 1981. Based
on this information you obtain a copy of her previous Notice of Admission, which is given below.

NOTICE OF ADMISSION (PREVIOUS)

1	Admitting No.	Date 7/17/81	Hosp. Empl. Initials	Soc. Sec. Number 707-36-5494	Suffix G		Case No. C-77-23071
		Is patient Medicare eligible?					

2	Patient's Name and Address (Last) Krebs (First) Giselle (Middle Initial)		Age 70	Patient's Birthdate 2/22/11	Sex F	Patient's Employer Green bria Garden

3	(No.) 1308 (Street) Ave R.	Name of Contract Holder S Krebs	Contract Holder's Employer Sandor's Nursery

4	(City) Brooklyn, (State) New York	Pat's relationship to Contract Holder: Self ☐ Spouse ☒ Dghtr ☐ Son ☐	Priv ☐ Semi Priv ☒ Priv ☐ ICU ☐

5	Full Name and Address of Physician Maurice J. Kellert 1844-48 Street, Bklyn, N.Y.	Was admission a result of auto accident? ☐ Yes ☒ No

6	Date Admitted Mo 7 Day 12 Year 81	Hour AM 7:15 PM	Admitting Diagnosis Stroke	Name and address of next of kin Julie Cohen 5625 Van Buren St Miami, Florida

7	Date Discharged CHECK ☐ Died ☒ Still in	Current or final diagnosis Stroke Was pregnancy terminated? ☐ No ☐ Yes	Relationship of next of kin to patient Daughter	Chart No. 414	Hospital Name Brooklyn Hospital	Hospital Code 8	Check Digit 14

Questions 5 through 8 refer to entries that would be made on the
current Notice of Admission shown on the next page. These entries
are to be based *SOLELY* on the information obtained from the patient
interview and the previous Notice of Admission given above.

NOTICE OF ADMISSION (CURRENT)

Admitting No.	Date	Hosp. Empl. Initials	Soc. Sec. Number	Suffix		Case No. C-
	Is patient Medicare eligible?					

Patient's Name and Address (Last) (First) (Middle Initial)	Age	Patient's Birthdate	Sex	Patient's Employer
(No.) (Street)	Name of Contract Holder		Contract Holder's Employer	
(City) (State)	Pat's. Relationship to Contract Holder Self Spouse Dghtr Son ☐ ☐ ☐ ☐		Priv. Semi Priv. Priv. Ward Icc ☐ ☐ ☐ ☐	

Full Name and Address of Physician	Was admission a result of auto accident? ☐ Yes ☐ No	
Date Admitted Mo. ¦ DAY ¦ YEAR	Hour A.M. ¦ P.M.	Admitting Diagnosis	Name and address of next of kin
Date Discharged	Current or final diagnosis	Relationship of next of kin to patient

CHECK	☐ Died ☐ Still in	Was pregnancy terminated? ☐ No ☐ Yes	Chart No.	Hospital Name	Hospital Code	Check Digit

5. *Which one* of the following lines on the current Notice of Admission could be completed based *SOLELY* on the information given in the Patient Interview on the previous Notice of Admission? (Assume that, unless otherwise specified, the information contained in the 1981 record remains the same.)   5. ...
   A. 4   B. 3   C. 5   D. 7

6. *Which one* of the following entries made on the previous Notice of Admission should *NOT* be transferred to the current Notice of Admission?   6. ...
   A. 1301 Avenue R, Brooklyn, New York
   B. 5025 Van Buren Street, Miami, Florida
   C. 2/22/11   D. 707-36-5491

7. *Which one* of the following entries would be the *same* on both Notices of Admission?   7. ...
   A. Sandor's Nursery   B. Stroke
   C. 7/12/74   D. Brooklyn Hospital

8. *Which one* of the following entries should *NOT* be made on Line 2 of the current Notice of Admission?   8. ...
   A. Green View Gardens   B. F   C. 70   D. 2/22/11

9

9. A patient's hospital bill is $27,200. The patient has   9. ...
   two different medical insurance plans, each of which will
   make partial payment toward her bill. One plan will pay
   the first $10,000 of the patient's bill, and the other
   will pay 50% of the remaining part of the bill not paid
   for by any other plan.
   The percentage of the entire bill paid for by the two
   plans is, most nearly,
   A. 64%   B. 66%   C. 68%   D. 70%

10. A hospital's daily rate is $285. This rate includes   10. ...
    all hospital services with the exception of blood, for
    which the hospital charges an additional $55 per pint.
    If a patient was charged for 17 days of hospitalization
    and the total hospital bill, including blood, was $5,285,
    how many pints of blood did the patient receive?
    A. 8   B. 9   C. 10   D. 11

Questions 11-12.
DIRECTIONS: Questions 11 and 12 are to be answered *SOLELY* on the
basis of the information shown below which indicates the charges
for hospital services and physician services given in a hospital
and a patient's annual income for each of four consecutive years.

YEAR	PATIENT'S ANNUAL INCOME	CHARGES FOR HOSPITAL SERVICES AND PHYSICIAN SERVICES GIVEN IN A HOSPITAL
1981	$14,000	$3,600
1982	$17,500	$4,250
1983	$18,600	$5,200
1984	$19,200	$5,850

11. A hospitalized patient may qualify for Medicaid benefits 11. ...
    when the charges for hospital services and for physician
    services given in the hospital exceed 30% of the patient's
    annual income.
    According to the information shown above, the *one* of the
    following that indicates *only* those years in which the
    patient qualifies for Medicaid benefits is
    A. 1983,1984   B. 1981,1983   C. 1982   D. 1984

12. The *one* of the following that is the patient's *average*   12. ...
    annual income for the entire four-year period shown above
    is
    A. $17,200   B. $17,300   C. $17,325   D. $17,525

Questions 13-14.
DIRECTIONS: Questions 13 and 14 are to be answered on the basis of
the information shown below, which gives the hospital bill and the
amount paid by an Insurance Plan for each of four patients.

PATIENT'S NAME	HOSPITAL BILL	AMOUNT PAID BY INSURANCE PLAN TOWARD HOSPITAL BILL
Mr. C. Minsky	$2,089	$1,890
Mr. S. Obrow	$6,823	$5,318
Ms. B. Kaet	$9,182	$8,000
Ms. D. Frieda	$7,633	$5,575

13. According to the information given above, *which* patient, 13. ...
    when compared with the other three patients, had the
    LOWEST percentage of his bill paid by the Insurance Plan?
    A. Mr. C. Minsky   B. Mr. S. Obrow
    C. Ms. B. Kaet   D. Ms. D. Frieda

14. The average amount of the hospital bills of the four   14. ...
    patients shown above is, most nearly,
      A. $6,334   B. $6,431   C. $6,481   D. $6,841
15. According to the provisions of the public health law,   15. ...
    rate schedules for city hospital services are based on
      A. per capita income of residents living in the area
         serviced by the hospital
      B. cost to the hospital of providing such services
      C. each patient's ability to pay
      D. gross family income of residents living in the
         area serviced by the hospital
16. *Which one* of the following statements best describes the 16. ...
    "no-fault" provisions of the State insurance law?
      A. No one person is truly to blame for any auto accident
      B. Regardless of fault in an auto accident, some in-
         surance will be provided to cover medical costs
      C. Passing a red light is not necessarily the fault of
         the driver
      D. If a pedestrian slips in front of a store, the store
         owner is not legally liable and is not to be held at
         fault
17. Assume that one of your cases has been in the hospital   17. ...
    for about six weeks due to an on-the-job injury. *Which
    one* of the following agencies should be *PRIMARILY* billed
    for his hospital stay?
      A. Bureau of Medical Assistance
      B. Crime Victims Compensation Board
      C. State Unemployment Bureau   D. Workmen's Compensation Board

Questions 18-20.
DIRECTIONS: Questions 18 through 20 are to be answered *SOLELY* on
the basis of the following information.

The White Cross Medical Plan provides covered-in-full benefits
for the first 24 days in any participating hospital. If a policyholder remains hospitalized or is readmitted for hospitalization,
the next 150 days are discount days, with the policyholder paying
40% of the hospital charges and the plan paying 60%.

A new benefit period of 24 days covered-in-full and 150 discount
days begins 60 days after completion of a previous hospital stay, or
after 270 continuous days of hospitalization. If the policyholder
uses up the entire covered-in-full and discount days without qualifying under the terms described above for a new benefit period, the
policyholder pays 100% of the hospital charges.

In the following questions, the patients are policyholders in
the medical plan described above and have had hospital stays at the
same participating hospital. The all-inclusive rate for services at
this hospital is $255 per day. In computing the length of a patient's
hospital stay, include the date the patient was admitted but do *NOT*
include the date the patient was discharged.

The calendar which follows should be used in answering the following questions.

1986

```
S M T W T F S          s m t w t f s                    S M T W T F S          s m t w t f s
JANUARY                APRIL                             JULY                   OCTOBER
        1  2  3  4             1  2  3  4  5                    1  2  3  4  5             1  2  3  4
 5  6  7  8  9 10 11     6  7  8  9 10 11 12              6  7  8  9 10 11 12     5  6  7  8  9 10 11
12 13 14 15 16 17 18    13 14 15 16 17 18 19             13 14 15 16 17 18 19    12 13 14 15 16 17 18
19 20 21 22 23 24 25    20 21 22 23 24 25 26             20 21 22 23 24 25 26    19 20 21 22 23 24 25
26 27 28 29 30 31       27 28 29 30                      27 28 29 30 31          26 27 28 29 30 31
FEBRUARY               MAY                              AUGUST      1  2         NOVEMBER              1
                 1              1  2  3                   3  4  5  6  7  8  9      2  3  4  5  6  7  8
 2  3  4  5  6  7  8     4  5  6  7  8  9 10             10 11 12 13 14 15 16     9 10 11 12 13 14 15
 9 10 11 12 13 14 15    11 12 13 14 15 16 17             17 18 19 20 21 22 23    16 17 18 19 20 21 22
16 17 18 19 20 21 22    18 19 20 21 22 23 24             24 25 26 27 28 29 30    23 24 25 26 27 28 29
23 24 25 26 27 28       25 26 27 28 29 30 31             31                      30
MARCH            1     JUNE                             SEPTEMBER               DECEMBER
 2  3  4  5  6  7  8     1  2  3  4  5  6  7                 1  2  3  4  5  6        1  2  3  4  5  6
 9 10 11 12 13 14 15     8  9 10 11 12 13 14              7  8  9 10 11 12 13      7  8  9 10 11 12 13
16 17 18 19 20 21 22    15 16 17 18 19 20 21             14 15 16 17 18 19 20    14 15 16 17 18 19 20
23 24 25 26 27 28 29    22 23 24 25 26 27 28             21 22 23 24 25 26 27    21 22 23 24 25 26 27
30 31                   29 30                            28 29 30                28 29 30 31
```

18. Mrs. Foley was admitted to the hospital on March 15,   18. ...
1986 and discharged on May 22, 1986. She was readmitted
on July 17, 1986 and discharged on July 26, 1986.
The total amount Mrs. Foley should pay for *BOTH* hospital
stays is, most nearly,
   A. $4,488   B. $5,046   C. $5,406   D. $5,610

19. Mr. Crane was admitted to the hospital on January 12,   19. ...
1986 and discharged on February 5, 1986. He was then
readmitted on June 5, 1986 and discharged on August 9,
1986.
The total amount Mr. Crane should pay for *BOTH* hospital
stays is, most nearly,
   A. $4,182   B. $6,273   C. $9,078   D. $10,455

20. Mr. Hayes was admitted to the hospital on October 20,   20. ...
1985 and discharged on December 4, 1986, having been
continuously hospitalized for a period of 410 days.
Assume that there are 365 days in a year and that
Mr. Hayes receives, at the completion of his hospital
stay, one bill that includes the charges for his total
hospitalization.
The amount that Mr. Hayes must pay the hospital is, most
nearly,
   A. $24,480   B. $39,780   C. $44,513   D. $51,612

KEY (CORRECT ANSWERS)

1. C		11. D
2. D		12. C
3. D		13. D
4. B		14. B
5. B		15. B
6. A		16. B
7. D		17. D
8. C		18. C
9. C		19. A
10. A		20. D

INTERVIEWING
EXAMINATION SECTION

DIRECTIONS FOR THIS SECTION:
Each question or incomplete statement is followed by several suggested answers or completions. Select the one that BEST answers the question or completes the statement. *PRINT THE LETTER OF THE CORRECT ANSWER IN THE SPACE AT THE RIGHT.*

TEST 1

1. Of the following, the MAIN advantage to the supervisor of using the indirect (or nondirective) interview, in which he asks only guiding questions and encourages the employee to do most of the talking, is that he can   1. ...
    A. obtain a mass of information about the employee in a very short period of time
    B. easily get at facts which the employee wishes to conceal
    C. get answers which are not slanted or biased in order to win his favor
    D. effectively deal with an employee's serious emotional problems

2. An interviewer under your supervision routinely closes his interview with a reassuring remark such as, "I'm sure you soon will be well," or "Everything will soon be all right." This practice is USUALLY considered   2. ...
    A. *advisable,* chiefly because the interviewer may make the patient feel better
    B. *inadvisable,* chiefly because it may cause a patient who is seriously ill to doubt the worker's understanding of the situation
    C. *advisable,* chiefly because the patient becomes more receptive if further interviews are needed
    D. *inadvisable,* chiefly because the interviewer should usually not show that he is emotionally involved

3. An interviewer has just ushered out a client he has interviewed. As the interviewer is preparing to leave, the client mentions a fact that seems to contradict the information he has given.
   Of the following, it would be BEST for the interviewer at this time to   3. ...
    A. make no response but write the fact down in his report and plan to come back another day
    B. point out to the client that he has contradicted himself and ask for an explanation
    C. ask the client to elaborate on the comment and attempt to find out further information about the fact
    D. disregard the comment since the client was probably exhausted and not thinking clearly

4. A client who is being interviewed insists on certain facts. The interviewer knows that these statements are incorrect. In regard to the rest of the client's statements, the interviewer is MOST justified to   4. ...
    A. disregard any information the client gives which cannot be verified
    B. try to discover other misstatements by confronting the client with the discrepancy
    C. consider everything else which the client has said as the truth unless proved otherwise

1

        D. ask the client to prove his statements

5. Immediately after the interviewer identifies himself to   5. ...
   a client, she says in a hysterical voice that she is not
   to be trusted.
   Of the following, the BEST course of action for the interviewer to follow would be to
      A. tell the woman sternly that if she does not stay calm,
        he will leave
      B. assure the woman that there is no cause to worry
      C. ignore the woman until she becomes quiet
      D. ask the woman to explain her problem

6. Assume that you are an interviewer and that one of your   6. ...
   interviewees has asked you for advice on dealing with a
   personal problem.
   Of the following, the BEST action for you to take is to
      A. tell him about a similar problem which you know
        worked out well
      B. advise him not to worry
      C. explain that the problem is quite a usual one and
        that the situation will be brighter soon
      D. give no opinion and change the subject when practicable

7. All of the following are, *generally*, good approaches for   7. ...
   an interviewer to use in order to improve his interviews
   EXCEPT
      A. developing a routine approach so that interviews can
        be standardized
      B. comparing his procedure with that of others engaged
        in similar work
      C. reviewing each interview critically, picking out one
        or two weak points to concentrate on improving
      D. comparing his own more successful and less successful
        interviews

8. Assume that a supervisor suggests at a staff meeting that   8. ...
   tape recording machines be provided for interviewers.
   Following are four arguments *against* the use of tape recorders that are raised by other members of the staff that
   might be valid:
     I. Recorded interviews provide too much unnecessary in-
       formation.
    II. Recorded interviews provide no record of manner or
       gestures.
   III. Tape recorders are too cumbersome and difficult for
       the average supervisor to manage.
    IV. Tape recorders may inhibit the interviewee.
   Which one of the following choices MOST accurately classi-
   fies the above into those which are generally *valid* and
   those which are *not?*
      A. I and II are generally valid, but III and IV are not.
      B. IV is generally valid, but I, II and III are not.
      C. I, II and IV are generally valid, but III is not.
      D. I, II, III and IV are generally valid.

9. During an interview the PRIMARY advantage of the technique   9. ...
   of using questions as opposed to allowing the interviewee
   to talk freely is that questioning
      A. gives the interviewer greater control
      B. provides a more complete picture

      C. makes the interviewee more relaxed

      D. decreases the opportunity for exaggeration

10. Assume that, in conducting an interview, an interviewer   10. ...
takes into consideration the age, sex, education, and
background of the subject.
This practice is GENERALLY considered
      A. *undesirable*, mainly because an interviewer may be
         prejudiced by such factors
      B. *desirable*, mainly because these are factors which
         might influence a person's response to certain questions
      C. *undesirable*, mainly because these factors rarely have
         any bearing on the matter being investigated
      D. *desirable*, mainly because certain categories of people
         answer certain questions in the same way

11. If a client should begin to tell his life story during an   11. ...
interview, the BEST course of action for an interviewer to
take is to
      A. interrupt immediately and insist that they return to
         business
      B. listen attentively until the client finishes and then
         ask if they can return to the subject
      C. pretend to have other business and come back later to
         see the client
      D. interrupt politely at an appropriate point and direct
         the client's attention to the subject

12. An interviewer who is trying to discover the circumstances 12. ...
surrounding a client's accident would be MOST successful
during an interview if he avoided questions which
      A. lead the client to discuss the matter in detail
      B. can easily be answered by either "yes" or "no"
      C. ask for specific information
      D. may be embarrassing or annoying to the client

13. A client being interviewed may develop an emotional re-   13. ...
action (positive or negative) toward the interviewer.
The BEST attitude for the interviewer to take toward
such feelings is that they are
      A. *inevitable;* they should be accepted but kept under
         control
      B. *unusual;* they should be treated impersonally
      C. *obstructive;* they should be resisted at all costs
      D. *abnormal;* they should be eliminated as soon as possible

14. Encouraging the client being interviewed to talk freely   14. ...
at first is a technique that is supported by all of the
following reasons EXCEPT that it
      A. tends to counteract any preconceived ideas that the
         interviewer may have entertained about the client
      B. gives the interviewer a chance to learn the best
         method of approach to obtain additional information
      C. inhibits the client from looking to the interviewer
         for support and advice
      D. allows the client to reveal the answers to many
         questions before they are asked

15. Of the following, *generally*, the MOST effective way for   15. ...
an interviewer to assure full cooperation from the client
he is interviewing is to
      A. sympathize with the client's problems and assure
         him of concern

3

B. tell a few jokes before beginning to ask questions
C. convince the patient that the answers to the questions will help him as well as the interviewer
D. arrange the interview when the client feels best

16. Since many elderly people are bewildered and helpless when interviewed, special consideration should be given to them.
Of the following, the BEST way for an interviewer to *initially* approach elderly clients who express anxiety and fear is to
A. assure them that they have nothing to worry about
B. listen patiently and show interest in them
C. point out the specific course of action that is best for them
D. explain to them that many people have overcome much greater difficulties

16. ...

17. Assume that, in planning an initial interview, an interviewer determines in advance what information is needed in order to fulfill the purpose of the interview.
Of the following, this procedure usually does NOT
A. reduce the number of additional interviews required
B. expedite the processing of the case
C. improve public opinion of the interviewer's agency
D. assure the cooperation of the person interviewed

17. ...

18. Sometimes an interviewer deliberately introduces his own personal interests and opinions into an interview with a client.
In general, this practice should be considered
A. *desirable,* primarily because the relationship between client and interviewer becomes social rather than businesslike
B. *undesirable,* primarily because the client might complain to his supervisor
C. *desirable;* primarily because the focus of attention is directed toward the client
D. *undesirable;* primarily because an argument between client and interviewer could result

18. ...

19. The one of the following types of interviewees who presents the LEAST difficult problem to handle is the person who
A. answers with a great many qualifications
B. talks at length about unrelated subjects so that the interviewer cannot ask questions
C. has difficulty understanding the interviewer's vocabulary
D. breaks into the middle of sentences and completes them with a meaning of his own

19. ...

20. A man being interviewed is entitled to Medicaid, but he refuses to sign up for it because he says he cannot accept any form of welfare.
Of the following, the *best* course of action for an interviewer to take FIRST is to
A. try to discover the reason for his feeling this way
B. tell him that he should be glad financial help is available

20. ...

4

      C. explain that others cannot help him if he will not
         help himself
      D. suggest that he speak to someone who is already on
         Medicaid

21. Of the following, the outcome of an interview by an inter- 21. ...
viewer depends MOST heavily on the
    A. personality of the interviewee
    B. personality of the interviewer
    C. subject matter of the questions asked
    D. interaction between interviewer and interviewee

22. Some clients being interviewed by an interviewer are   22. ...
primarily interested in making a favorable impression.
The interviewer should be aware of the fact that such
clients are MORE likely than *other* clients to
    A. try to anticipate the answers the interviewer is
       looking for
    B. answer all questions openly and frankly
    C. try to assume the role of interviewer
    D. be anxious to get the interview over as quickly as
       possible

23. The type of interview which a hospital care interviewer 23. ...
usually conducts is *substantially different* from most
interviewing situations in all of the following aspects
EXCEPT the
    A. setting   B. kinds of clients
    C. techniques employed   D. kinds of problems

24. During an interview, an interviewer uses a "leading ques- 24. ...
tion."
This type of question is so-called because it, *generally*,
    A. starts a series of questions about one topic
    B. suggests the answer which the interviewer wants
    C. forms the basis for a following "trick" question
    D. sets, at the beginning, the tone of the interview

25. An interviewer may face various difficulties when he tries 25. ...
to obtain information from a client.
Of the following, the difficulty which is EASIEST for the
interviewer to *overcome* occurs when a client
    A. is unwilling to reveal the information
    B. misunderstands what information is needed
    C. does not have the information available to him
    D. is unable to coherently give the information requested

TEST 2

1. Of the following, the MOST appropriate manner for an in-   1. ...
terviewer to assume during an interview with a client is
    A. authoritarian B. paternal C. casual D. businesslike

2. The systematic study of interviewing theory, principles   2. ...
and techniques by an interviewer will, *usually*,
    A. aid him to act in a depersonalized manner
    B. turn his interviewes into stereotyped affairs
    C. make the people he interviews feel manipulated
    D. give him a basis for critically examining his own
       practice

3. Compiling in advance a list of general questions to ask a   3. ...
   client during an interview is a technique *usually* considered
      A. *desirable,* chiefly because reference to the list will
         help keep the interview focused on the important issues
      B. *undesirable,* chiefly because use of such a list will
         discourage the client from speaking freely
      C. *desirable,* chiefly because the list will serve as a
         record of what questions were asked
      D. *undesirable,* chiefly because use of such a list will
         make the interview too mechanical and impersonal

4. The one of the following which is usually of GREATEST   4. ...
   importance in winning the cooperation of a person being
   interviewed while achieving the purpose of the interview
   is the interviewer's ability to
      A. gain the confidence of the person being interviewed
      B. stick to the subject of the interview
      C. handle a person who is obviously lying
      D. prevent the person being interviewed from withholding
         information

5. While interviewing clients, an interviewer should use the   5. ...
   technique of interruption, beginning to speak when a client
   has temporarily paused at the end of a phrase or sentence,
   in order to
      A. limit the client's ability to voice his objections
         or complaints
      B. shorten, terminate or redirect a client's response
      C. assert authority when he feels that the client is too
         conceited
      D. demonstrate to the client that pauses in speech should
         be avoided

6. An interviewer might gain background information about a   6. ...
   client by being aware of the person's speech during an
   interview.
   Which one of the following patterns of speech would offer
   the LEAST accurate information about a client? The
      A. number of slang expressions and the level of vocabulary
      B. presence and degree of an accent
      C. rate of speech and the audibility level
      D. presence of a physical speech defect

7. Suppose that you are interviewing a distressed client who   7. ...
   claims that he was just laid off from his job and has no
   money to pay his rent.
   Your FIRST action should be to
      A. ask if he has sought other employment or has other
         sources of income
      B. express your sympathy but explain that he must pay
         the rent on time
      C. inquire about the reasons he was laid off from work
      D. try to transfer him to a smaller apartment which he
         can afford

8. Suppose you have some background information on an appli-   8. ...
   cant whom you are interviewing. During the interview it
   appears that the applicant is giving you *false* information.
   The BEST thing for you to do at that point is to
      A. pretend that you are not aware of the written facts
         and let him continue

    B. tell him what you already know and discuss the dis-
       crepancies with him

    C. terminate the interview and make a note that the
       applicant is untrustworthy

    D. tell him that, because he is making false statements,
       he will not be eligible for an apartment

9. A Spanish-speaking applicant may want to bring his bilin-   9. ...
gual child with him to an interview to act as an interpreter.
Which of the following would be LEAST likely to affect the
value of an interview in which an applicant's child has
acted as interpreter?

    A. It may make it undesirable to ask certain questions.

    B. A child may do an inadequate job of interpretation.

    C. A child's answers may indicate his feelings toward
       his parents.

    D. The applicant may not want to reveal all information
       in front of his child.

10. Assume you are assigned to interview applicants.   10. ...
Of the following, which is the BEST attitude for you to
take in dealing with applicants?

    A. Assume they will enjoy being interviewed because they
       believe that you have the power of decision

    B. Expect that they have a history of anti-social behav-
       ior in the family, and probe deeply into the social
       development of family members

    C. Expect that they will try to control the interview,
       thus you should keep them on the defensive

    D. Assume that they will be polite and cooperative and
       attempt to secure the information you need in a
       business-like manner

11. If you are interviewing an applicant who is a minority   11. ...
group member in reference to his eligibility, it would
be BEST for you to use language that is

    A. *informal*, using ethnic expressions known to the
       applicant

    B. *technical*, using the expressions commonly used in
       the agency

    C. *simple*, using words and phrases which laymen understand

    D. *formal*, to remind the applicant that he is dealing with
       a government agency

12. When interviewing an applicant to determine his eligibil-   12. ...
ity, it is MOST important to

    A. have a prior mental picture of the typical eligible
       applicant

    B. conduct the interview strictly according to a previous-
       ly prepared script

    C. keep in mind the goal of the interview, which is to
       determine eligibility

    D. get an accurate and detailed account of the applicant's
       life history

13. The practice of trying to imagine yourself in the appli-   13. ...
cant's place during an interview is

    A. *good*; mainly because you will be able to evaluate his
       responses better

    B. *good*; mainly because it will enable you to treat him
       as a friend rather than as an applicant

C. *poor;* mainly because it is important for the applicant to see you as an impartial person
D. *poor;* mainly because it is too time-consuming to do
this with each applicant

14. When dealing with clients from different ethnic back-   14. ...
grounds, you should be aware of certain tendencies toward
prejudice.
Which of the following statements is LEAST likely to be
valid?
A. Whites prejudiced against blacks are more likely to
be prejudiced against Puerto Ricans than whites not
prejudiced against blacks.
B. The less a white is in competition with blacks, the
less likely he is to be prejudiced against them.
C. Persons who have moved from one social group to
another are likely to retain the attitudes and prej-
udices of their original social group.
D. When there are few blacks or Puerto Ricans in a
project, whites are less likely to be prejudiced
against them than when there are many.

15. Of the following, the one who is MOST likely to be a good 15. ...
interviewer of people seeking assistance, is one who
A. tries to get applicants to apply to another agency
instead
B. believes that it is necessary to get as much pertinent
information as possible in order to determine the applicant's real needs
C. believes that people who seek assistance are likely to
have persons with a history of irresponsible behavior
in their households
D. is convinced that there is no need for a request for
assistance

KEYS (CORRECT ANSWERS)

TEST 1				TEST 2	
1.	C	11.	D	1.	D
2.	B	12.	B	2.	D
3.	C	13.	A	3.	A
4.	C	14.	C	4.	A
5.	D	15.	C	5.	B
6.	D	16.	B	6.	C
7.	A	17.	D	7.	A
8.	C	18.	D	8.	B
9.	A	19.	C	9.	C
10.	B	20.	A	10.	D
		21.	D		
		22.	A	11.	C
		23.	C	12.	C
		24.	B	13.	A
		25.	B	14.	C
				15.	B

READING COMPREHENSION
UNDERSTANDING AND INTERPRETING WRITTEN MATERIAL
EXAMINATION SECTION
TEST 1

Questions 1-8.

DIRECTIONS: Each question or incomplete statement is followed by several suggested answers or completions. Select the one that BEST answers the question or completes the statement. *PRINT THE LETTER OF THE CORRECT ANSWER IN THE SPACE AT THE RIGHT.*

Questions 1 and 2.

DIRECTIONS: Your answers to Questions 1 and 2 must be based ONLY on the information given in the following paragraph.

Hospitals maintained wholly by public taxation may treat only those compensation cases which are emergencies and may not treat such emergency cases longer than the emergency exists; provided, however, that these restrictions shall not be applicable where there is not available a hospital other than a hospital maintained wholly by taxation.

1. According to the above paragraph, compensation cases   1.___
   A. are regarded as emergency cases by hospitals maintained wholly by public taxation
   B. are seldom treated by hospitals maintained wholly by public taxation
   C. are treated mainly by privately endowed hospitals
   D. may be treated by hospitals maintained wholly by public taxation if they are emergencies

2. According to the above paragraph, it is MOST reasonable to   2.___
   conclude that where a privately endowed hospital is available,
   A. a hospital supported wholly by public taxation may treat emergency compensation cases only so long as the emergency exists
   B. a hospital supported wholly by public taxation may treat any compensation cases
   C. a hospital supported wholly by public taxation must refer emergency compensation cases to such a hospital
   D. the restrictions regarding the treatment of compensation cases by a tax-supported hospital are not wholly applicable

Questions 3-7.

DIRECTIONS: Answer Questions 3 through 7 ONLY according to the information given in the following passage.

THE MANUFACTURE OF LAUNDRY SOAP

The manufacture of soap is not a complicated process. Soap is a fat or an oil, plus an alkali, water and salt. The alkali used in making commercial laundry soap is caustic soda. The salt used is the same as common table salt. A fat is generally an animal product that is not a liquid at room temperature. If heated, it becomes a liquid. An oil is generally liquid at room temperature. If the temperature is lowered, the oil becomes a solid just like ordinary fat.

At the soap plant, a huge tank five stories high, called a *kettle*, is first filled part way with fats and then the alkali and water are added. These ingredients are then heated and boiled together. Salt is then poured into the top of the boiling solution; and as the salt slowly sinks down through the mixture, it takes with it the glycerine which comes from the melted fats. The product which finally comes from the kettle is a clear soap which has a moisture content of about 34%. This clear soap is then chilled so that more moisture is driven out. As a result, the manufacturer finally ends up with a commercial laundry soap consisting of 88% clear soap and only 12% moisture.

3. An ingredient used in making laundry soap is   3.___
    A. table sugar   B. potash
    C. glycerine   D. caustic soda

4. According to the above passage, a difference between fats   4.___
   and oils is that fats
    A. cost more than oils
    B. are solid at room temperature
    C. have less water than oils
    D. are a liquid animal product

5. According to the above passage, the MAIN reason for using   5.___
   salt in the manufacture of soap is to
    A. make the ingredients boil together
    B. keep the fats in the kettle melted
    C. remove the glycerine
    D. prevent the loss of water from the soap

6. According to the passage, the purpose of chilling the clear   6.___
   soap is to
    A. stop the glycerine from melting
    B. separate the alkali from the fats
    C. make the oil become solid
    D. get rid of more moisture

7. According to the passage, the percentage of moisture in   7.___
   commercial laundry soap is
    A. 12%   B. 34%   C. 66%   D. 88%

8. The x-ray has gone into business. Developed primarily to   8.___
   aid in diagnosing human ills, the machine now works in packing
   plants, in foundries, in service stations, and in a dozen ways
   to contribute to precision and accuracy in industry.
   The above statement means *most nearly* that the x-ray
   A. was first developed to aid business
   B. is of more help to business than it is to medicine
   C. is being used to improve the functioning of business
   D. is more accurate for packing plants than it is for
      foundries

Questions 9-25.

DIRECTIONS: Each question consists of a statement. You are to
              indicate whether the statement is TRUE (T) or FALSE (F).
              *PRINT THE LETTER OF THE CORRECT ANSWER IN THE SPACE AT
              THE RIGHT.*

Questions 9-12.

DIRECTIONS: Read the paragraph below about *shock* and then answer
              Questions 9 through 12 according to the information
              given in the paragraph.

<u>SHOCK</u>

   While not found in all injuries, shock is present in all serious
injuries caused by accidents. During shock, the normal activities of
the body slow down. This partly explains why one of the signs of shock
is a pale, cold skin, since insufficient blood goes to the body parts
during shock.

9. If the injury caused by an accident is serious, shock is   9.___
   sure to be present.

10. In shock, the heart beats faster than normal.   10.___

11. The face of a person suffering from shock is usually red   11.___
    and flushed.

12. Not enough blood goes to different parts of the body during   12.___
    shock.

Questions 13-18.

DIRECTIONS: Questions 13 through 18, inclusive, are to be answered
              SOLELY on the basis of the information contained in the
              following statement and NOT upon any other information
              you may have.

   Blood transfusions are given to patients at the hospital upon
recommendation of the physicians attending such cases. The physician
fills out a *Request for Blood Transfusion* form in duplicate and sends
both copies to the Medical Director's office, where a list is maintained of persons called *donors* who desire to sell their blood for

transfusions. A suitable donor is selected, and the transfusion is given. Donors are, in many instances, medical students and employees of the hospital. Donors receive twenty-five dollars for each transfusion.

13. According to the above paragraph, a blood donor is paid   13.__
    twenty-five dollars for each transfusion.

14. According to the above paragraph, only medical students and   14.__
    employees of the hospital are selected as blood donors.

15. According to the above paragraph, the *Request for Blood*   15.__
    Transfusion form is filled out by the patient and sent to
    the Medical Director's office.

16. According to the above paragraph, a list of blood donors is   16.__
    maintained in the Medical Director's office.

17. According to the above paragraph, cases for which the   17.__
    attending physicians recommend blood transfusions are
    usually emergency cases.

18. According to the above paragraph, one copy of the *Request*   18.__
    for Blood Transfusion form is kept by the patient and one
    copy is sent to the Medical Director's office.

Questions 19-25.

DIRECTIONS: Questions 19 through 25, inclusive, are to be answered
              SOLELY on the basis of the information contained in the
              following statement and NOT upon any other information
              you may have.

Before being admitted to a hospital ward, a patient is first interviewed by the Admitting Clerk, who records the patient's name, age, sex, race, birthplace, and mother's maiden name. This clerk takes all of the money and valuables that the patient has on his person. A list of the valuables is written on the back of the envelope in which the valuables are afterwards placed. Cash is counted and placed in a separate envelope, and the amount of money and the name of the patient are written on the outside of the envelope. Both envelopes are sealed, fastened together, and placed in a compartment of a safe.

An orderly then escorts the patient to a dressing room where the patient's clothes are removed and placed in a bundle. A tag bearing the patient's name is fastened to the bundle. A list of the contents of the bundle is written on property slips, which are made out in triplicate. The information contained on the outside of the envelopes containing the cash and valuables belonging to the patient is also copied on the property slips.

According to the above paragraph,

19. patients are escorted to the dressing room by the Admitting   19.__
    Clerk.

20. the patient's cash and valuables are placed together in one envelope. 20.____

21. the number of identical property slips that are made out when a patient is being admitted to a hospital ward is three. 21.____

22. the full names of both parents of a patient are recorded by the Admitting Clerk before a patient is admitted to a hospital ward. 22.____

23. the amount of money that a patient has on his person when admitted to the hospital is entered on the patient's property slips. 23.____

24. an orderly takes all the money and valuables that a patient has on his person. 24.____

25. the patient's name is placed on the tag that is attached to the bundle containing the patient's clothing. 25.____

KEY (CORRECT ANSWERS)

1. D		11. F	
2. A		12. T	
3. D		13. T	
4. B		14. F	
5. C		15. F	
6. D		16. T	
7. A		17. T	
8. C		18. F	
9. T		19. F	
10. F		20. F	

21. T
22. F
23. T
24. F
25. T

TEST 2

DIRECTIONS: Each question or incomplete statement is followed by several suggested answers or completions. Select the one that BEST answers the question or completes the statement. *PRINT THE LETTER OF THE CORRECT ANSWER IN THE SPACE AT THE RIGHT.*

Questions 1-4.

DIRECTIONS: Questions 1 through 4 are to be answered in accordance with the following paragraphs.

One fundamental difference between the United States health care system and the health care systems of some European countries is the way that hospital charges for long-term illnesses affect their citizens.

In European countries such as England, Sweden, and Germany, citizens can face, without fear, hospital charges due to prolonged illness, no matter how substantial they may be. Citizens of these nations are required to pay nothing when they are hospitalized, for they have prepaid their treatment as taxpayers when they were well and were earning incomes.

On the other hand, the United States citizen, in spite of the growth of payments by third parties which include private insurance carriers as well as public resources, has still to shoulder 40 percent of hospital care costs, while his private insurance contributes only 25 percent and public resources the remaining 35 percent. Despite expansion of private health insurance and social legislation in the United States, out-of-pocket payments for hospital care by individuals have steadily increased. Such payments, currently totalling $23 billion, are nearly twice as high as ten years ago.

Reform is inevitable and, when it comes, will have to reconcile sharply conflicting interests. Hospital staffs are demanding higher and higher wages. Hospitals are under pressure by citizens, who as patients demand more and better services but who as taxpayers or as subscribers to hospital insurance plans, are reluctant to pay the higher cost of improved care. An acceptable reconciliation of these interests has so far eluded legislators and health administrators in the United States.

1. According to the above passage, the one of the following which is an ADVANTAGE that citizens of England, Sweden, and Germany have over United States citizens is that, when faced with long-term illness,   1.___
   A. the amount of out-of-pocket payments made by these European citizens is small when compared to out-of-pocket payments made by United States citizens
   B. European citizens have no fear of hospital costs no matter how great they may be

    C. more efficient and reliable hospitals are available
       to the European citizen than is available to the
       United States citizens
    D. a greater range of specialized hospital care is
       available to the European citizens than is available
       to the United States citizens

2. According to the above passage, reform of the United   2.___
   States system of health care must reconcile all of the
   following EXCEPT
    A. attempts by health administrators to provide improved
       hospital care
    B. taxpayers' reluctance to pay for the cost of more
       and better hospital services
    C. demands by hospital personnel for higher wages
    D. insurance subscribers' reluctance to pay the higher
       costs of improved hospital care

3. According to the above passage, the out-of-pocket payments 3.___
   for hospital care that individuals made ten years ago was
   APPROXIMATELY ____ billion.
    A. $32   B. $23   C. $12   D. $3

4. According to the above passage, the GREATEST share of   4.___
   the costs of hospital care in the United States is paid by
    A. United States citizens   B. private insurance carriers
    C. public resources   D. third parties

Questions 5-8.

DIRECTIONS: Questions 5 through 8 are to be answered SOLELY on the
            basis of the information contained in the following passage.

    Effective cost controls have been difficult to establish in most
hospitals in the United States. Ways must be found to operate hospitals with reasonable efficiency without sacrificing quality and in a
manner that will reduce the amount of personal income now being spent
on health care and the enormous drain on national resources. We must
adopt a new public objective of providing higher quality health care
at significantly lower cost. One step that can be taken to achieve
this goal is to carefully control capital expenditures for hospital
construction and expansion. Perhaps the way to start is to declare
a moratorium on all hospital construction and to determine the
factors that should be considered in deciding whether a hospital
should be built. Such factors might include population growth,
distance to the nearest hospital, availability of medical personnel,
and hospital bed shortage.

    A second step to achieve the new objective is to increase the
ratio of out-of-hospital patient to in-hospital patient care. This
can be done by using separate health care facilities other than
hospitals to attract patients who have increasingly been going to
hospital clinics and overcrowding them. Patients should instead
identify with a separate health care facility to keep them out of
hospitals.

A third step is to require better hospital operating rules and controls. This step might include the review of a doctor's performance by other doctors, outside professional evaluations of medical practice, and required refresher courses and re-examinations for doctors. Other measures might include obtaining mandatory second opinions on the need for surgery in order to avoid unnecessary surgery, and outside review of work rules and procedures to eliminate unnecessary testing of patients.

A fourth step is to halt the construction and public subsidizing of new medical schools and to fill whatever needs exist in professional coverage by emphasizing the medical training of physicians with specialities that are in short supply and by providing a better geographic distribution of physicians and surgeons.

5. According to the above passage, providing higher quality   5.___
   health care at lower cost can be achieved by the
   A. greater use of out-of-hospital facilities
   B. application of more effective cost controls on doctors'
      fees
   C. expansion of improved in-hospital patient care services
      at hospital clinics
   D. development of more effective training programs in
      hospital administration

6. According to the above passage, the one of the following   6.___
   which should be taken into account in determining if a
   hospital should be constructed is the
   A. number of out-of-hospital health care facilities
   B. availability of public funds to subsidize construction
   C. number of hospitals under construction
   D. availability of medical personnel

7. According to the above passage, it is IMPORTANT to   7.___
   operate hospitals efficiently because
   A. they are currently in serious financial difficulties
   B. of the need to reduce the amount of personal income
      going to health care
   C. the quality of health care services has deteriorated
   D. of the need to increase productivity goals to take
      care of the growing population in the United States

8. According to the above passage, which one of the   8.___
   following approaches is MOST LIKELY to result in better
   operating rules and controls in hospitals?
   A. Allocating doctors to health care facilities on the
      basis of patient population
   B. Equalizing the workloads of doctors
   C. Establishing a physician review board to evaluate
      the performance of other physicians
   D. Eliminating unnecessary outside review of patient
      testing

Questions 9-14.

DIRECTIONS: Questions 9 through 14 are to be answered SOLELY on the basis of the information contained in the following passage.

The United States today is the only major industrial nation in the world without a system of national health insurance or a national health service. Instead, we have placed our prime reliance on private enterprise and private health insurance to meet the need. Yet, in a recent year, of the 180 million Americans under 65 years of age, 34 million had no hospital insurance, 38 million had no surgical insurance, 63 million had no out-patient x-ray and laboratory insurance, 94 million had no insurance for prescription drugs, and 103 million had no insurance for physician office visits or home visits. Some 35 million Americans under the age of 65 had no health insurance whatsoever. Some 64 million additional Americans under age 65 had health insurance coverage that was less than that provided to the aged under Medicare.

Despite more than three decades of enormous growth, the private health insurance industry today pays benefits equal to only one-third of the total cost of private health care, leaving the rest to be borne by the patient - essentially the same ratio which held true a decade ago. Moreover, nearly all private health insurance is limited; it provides partial benefits, not comprehensive benefits; acute care, not preventive care; it siphons off the young and healthy, and ignores the poor and medically indigent. The typical private carrier usually pays only the cost of hospital care, forcing physicians and patients alike to resort to wasteful and inefficient use of hospital facilities, thereby giving further impetus to the already soaring costs of hospital care. Valuable hospital beds are used for routine tests and examinations. Unnecessary hospitalization, unnecessary surgery, and unnecessarily extended hospital stays are encouraged. These problems are exacerbated by the fact that administrative costs of commercial carriers are substantially higher than they are for Blue Shield, Blue Cross, or Medicare.

9. According to the above passage, the PROPORTION of total private health care costs paid by private health insurance companies today as compared to ten years ago has   9.___
   A. *increased* by approximately one-third
   B. *remained* practically the same
   C. *increased* by approximately two-thirds
   D. *decreased* by approximately one-third

10. According to the above passage, the one of the following which has contributed MOST to wasteful use of hospital facilities is the   10.___
   A. increased emphasis on preventive health care
   B. practice of private carriers of providing comprehensive health care benefits
   C. increased hospitalization of the elderly and the poor
   D. practice of a number of private carriers of paying only for hospital care costs

11. Based on the information in the above passage, which one   11.___
    of the following patients would be LEAST likely to receive
    benefits from a typical private health insurance plan?
    A
       A. young patient who must undergo an emergency appendec-
          tomy
       B. middle-aged patient who needs a costly series of
          x-ray and laboratory tests for diagnosis of gastro-
          intestinal complaints
       C. young patient who must visit his physician weekly ·
          for treatment of a chronic skin disease
       D. middle-aged patient who requires extensive cancer
          surgery

12. Which one of the following is the MOST accurate inference   12.___
    that can be drawn from the above passage?
       A. Private health insurance has failed to fully meet the
          health care needs of Americans.
       B. Most Americans under age 65 have health insurance
          coverage better than that provided to the elderly
          under Medicare.
       C. Countries with a national health service are likely
          to provide poorer health care for their citizens than
          do countries that rely primarily on private health
          insurance.
       D. Hospital facilities in the United States are inade-
          quate to meet the nation's health care needs.

13. Of the total number of Americans under age 65, what   13.___
    percentage belonged in the combined category of persons
    with NO health insurance or health insurance less than
    that provided to the aged under Medicare?
       A. 19%   B. 36%   C. 55%   D. 65%

14. According to the above passage, the one of the following   14.___
    types of health insurance which covered the SMALLEST
    number of Americans under age 65 was
       A. hospital insurance
       B. surgical insurance
       C. insurance for prescription drugs
       D. insurance for physician office or home visits

Questions 15-17.

DIRECTIONS: Questions 15 through 17 are to be answered SOLELY on the
             basis of the information contained in the following
             passage.

     Statistical studies have demonstrated that disease and mortality
rates are higher among the poor than among the more affluent members
of our society. Periodic surveys conducted by the United States Public
Health Service continue to document a higher prevalence of infectious
and chronic diseases within low income families. While the basic life
style and living conditions of the poor are to a considerable extent
responsible for this less favorable health status, there are indica-
tions that the kind of health care received by the poor also plays a

significant role. The poor are less likely to be aware of the concepts and practices of scientific medicine and less likely to seek health care when they need it. Moreover, they are discouraged from seeking adequate health care by the depersonalization, disorganization, and inadequate emphasis on preventive care which characterize the health care most often provided for them.

To achieve the objective of better health care for the poor, the following approaches have been suggested: encouraging the poor to seek preventive care as well as care for acute illness and to establish a lasting one-to-one relationship with a single physician who can treat the poor patient as a whole individual; sufficient financial subsidy to put the poor on an equal footing with *paying patients*, thereby giving them the opportunity to choose from among available health services providers; inducements to health services providers to establish public clinics in poverty areas; and legislation to provide for health education, earlier detection of disease, and coordinated health care.

15. According to the above passage, the one of the following   15.___
     which is a function of the United States Public Health
     Service is
         A. gathering data on the incidence of infectious diseases
         B. operating public health clinics in poverty areas lacking
            private physicians
         C. recommending legislation for the improvement of health
            care in the United States
         D. encouraging the poor to participate in programs aimed
            at the prevention of illness

16. According to the above passage, the one of the following   16.___
     which is MOST characteristic of the health care currently
     provided for the poor is that it
         A. aims at establishing clinics in poverty areas
         B. enables the poor to select the health care they want
            through the use of financial subsidies
         C. places insufficient stress on preventive health care
         D. over-emphasizes the establishment of a one-to-one
            relationship between physician and patient

17. The above passage IMPLIES that the poor lack the financial   17.___
     resources to
         A. obtain adequate health insurance coverage
         B. select from among existing health services
         C. participate in health education programs
         D. lobby for legislation aimed at improving their
            health care

Questions 18-20.

DIRECTIONS: Questions 18 through 20 are to be answered SOLELY on the
basis of the information contained in the following
passage.

The concept of *affiliation*, developed more than ten years ago,
grew out of a series of studies which found evidence of faulty care,
surgery of *questionable* value and other undesirable conditions in
the city's municipal hospitals. The affiliation agreements ·signed
shortly thereafter were designed to correct these deficiencies by
assuring high quality medical care. · In general, the agreements
provided the staff and expertise of a voluntary hospital - sometimes
connected with a medical school - to operate various services or,
in some cases, all of the professional divisions of a specific
municipal hospital. The municipal hospitals have paid for these
services, which last year cost the city $200 million, the largest
single expenditure of the Health and Hospitals Corporation. In
addition, the municipal hospitals have provided to the voluntary
hospitals such facilities as free space for laboratories and research.
While some experts agree that affiliation has resulted in improvements
in some hospital care, they contend that many conditions that affiliation was meant to correct still exist. In addition, accountability
procedures between the Corporation and voluntary hospitals are said
to be so inadequate that audits of affiliation contracts of the past
five years revealed that there may be more than $200 million in
charges for services by the voluntary hospitals which have not been
fully substantiated. Consequently, the Corporation has proposed
that future agreements provide accountability in terms of funds,
services supplied, and use of facilities by the voluntary hospitals.

18.   According to the above passage, *affiliation* may BEST be   18.___
      defined as an agreement whereby
         A. voluntary hospitals pay for the use of municipal
            hospital facilities
         B. voluntary and municipal hospitals work to eliminate
            duplication of services
         C. municipal hospitals pay voluntary hospitals for
            services performed
         D. voluntary and municipal hospitals transfer patients
            to take advantage of specialized ·services

19.   According to the above passage, the MAIN purpose for   19.___
      setting up the *affiliation* agreement was to
         A. supplement the revenues of municipal hospitals
         B. improve the quality of medical care in municipal
            hospitals
         C. reduce operating costs in municipal hospitals
         D. increase the amount of space available to municipal
            hospitals

20.   According to the above passage, inadequate accountability   20.___
      procedures have resulted in
         A. unsubstantiated charges for services by the voluntary
            hospitals

B. emphasis on research rather than on patient care in municipal hospitals
C. unsubstantiated charges for services by the municipal hospitals
D. economic losses to voluntary hospitals

Questions 21-25.

DIRECTIONS: Questions 21 through 25 are to be answered SOLELY on the basis of the information contained in the following passage.

The payment for medical services covered under the Outpatient Medical Insurance Plan (OMI) may be made, by OMI, directly to a physician or to the OMI patient. If the physician and the patient agree that the physician is to receive payment directly from OMI, the payment will be officially assigned to the physician; this is the assignment method. If payment is not assigned, the patient receives payment directly from OMI based on an itemized bill he submits, regardless of whether or not he has already paid his physician.

When a physician accepts assignment of the payment for medical services, he agrees that total charges will not be more than the allowed charge determined by the OMI carrier administering the program. In such cases, the OMI patient pays any unmet part of the $85 annual deductible, plus 10 percent of the remaining charges to the physician. In unassigned claims, the patient is responsible for the total amount charged by the physician. The patient will then be reimbursed by the program 90 percent of the allowed charges in excess of the annual deductible.

The rates of acceptance of assignments provide a measure of how many OMI patients are spared *administrative participation* in the program. Because physicians are free to accept or reject assignments, the rate in which assignments are made provide a general indication of the medical community's satisfaction with the OMI program, especially with the level of amounts paid by the program for specific services and the promptness of payment.

21. According to the above passage, in order for a physician   21.___
to receive payment directly from OMI for medical services
to an OMI patient, the physician would have to accept the
assignment of payment, to have the consent of the patient,
AND to
A. submit to OMI a paid itemized bill
B. collect from the patient 90% of the total bill
C. collect from the patient the total amount of the
charges for his services, a portion of which he
will later reimburse the patient
D. agree that his charges for services to the patient
will not exceed the amount allowed by the program

22. According to the above passage, if a physician accepts assignment of payment, the patient pays
    A. the total amount charged by the physician and is reimbursed by the program for 90 percent of the allowed charges in excess of the applicable deductible
    B. any unmet part of the $85 annual deductible, plus 90 percent of the remaining charges
    C. the total amount charged by the physician and is reimbursed by the program for 10 percent of the allowed charges in excess of the $85 annual deductible
    D. any unmet part of the $85 annual deductible, plus 10 percent of the remaining charges

22.___

23. A physician has accepted the assignment of payment for charges to an OMI patient. The physician's charges, all of which are allowed under OMI, amount to $115. This is the first time the patient has been eligible for OMI benefits and the first time the patient has received services from this physician.
    According to the above passage, the patient must pay the physician
    A. $27   B. $76.50   C. $88   D. $103.50

23.___

24. In an unassigned claim, a physician's charges, all of which are allowed under OMI, amount to $165. The patient paid the physician the full amount of the bill.
    If this is the FIRST time the patient has been eligible for OMI benefits, he will receive from OMI a reimbursement of
    A. $72   B. $80   C. $85   D. $93

24.___

25. According to the above passage, if the rate of acceptance of assignments by physicians is high, it is LEAST appropriate to conclude that the medical community is generally satisfied with the
    A. supplementary medical insurance program
    B. levels of amounts paid to physicians by the program
    C. number of OMI patients being spared administrative participation in the program
    D. promptness of the program in making payment for services

25.___

KEY (CORRECT ANSWERS)

1. B	6. D	11. C	16. C	21. D
2. A	7. B	12. A	17. B	22. D
3. C	8. C	13. C	18. C	23. C
4. D	9. B	14. D	19. B	24. A
5. A	10. D	15. A	20. A	25. C

READING COMPREHENSION
UNDERSTANDING AND INTERPRETING WRITTEN MATERIAL
EXAMINATION SECTION

DIRECTIONS: Each question or incomplete statement is followed by several suggested answers or completions. Select the one that BEST answers the question or completes the statement. *PRINT THE LETTER OF THE CORRECT ANSWER IN THE SPACE AT THE RIGHT.*

TEST 1

Questions 1-5.

DIRECTIONS: Questions 1 through 5 are to be answered SOLELY on the basis of the following passage.

The most effective control mechanism to prevent gross incompetence on the part of public employees is a good personnel program. The personnel officer in the line departments and the central personnel agency should exert positive leadership to raise levels of performance. Although the key factor is the quality of the personnel recruited, staff members other than personnel officers can make important contributions to efficiency. Administrative analysts, now employed in many agencies, make detailed studies of organization and procedures, with the purpose of eliminating delays, waste, and other inefficiencies. Efficiency is, however, more than a question of good organization and procedures; it is also the product of the attitudes and values of the public employees. Personal motivation can provide the will to be efficient. The best management studies will not result in substantial improvement of the performance of those employees who feel no great urge to work up to their abilities.

1. The above passage indicates that the KEY factor in prevent-   1.___
    ing gross incompetence of public employees is the
    A. hiring of administrative analysts to assist personnel
       people
    B. utilization of effective management studies
    C. overlapping of responsibility
    D. quality of the employees hired

2. According to the above passage, the central personnel   2.___
    agency staff SHOULD
    A. work more closely with administrative analysts in
       the line departments than with personnel officers
    B. make a serious effort to avoid jurisdictional con-
       flicts with personnel officers in line departments
    C. contribute to improving the quality of work of
       public employees
    D. engage in a comprehensive program to change the
       public's negative image of public employees

3. The above passage indicates that efficiency in an organi-   3.___
    zation can BEST be brought about by
    A. eliminating ineffective control mechanisms

        B. instituting sound organizational procedures
        C. promoting competent personnel
        D. recruiting people with desire to do good work

  4. According to the above passage, the purpose of administra-   4.___
     tive analysis in a public agency is to
        A. prevent injustice to the public employee
        B. promote the efficiency of the agency
        C. protect the interests of the public
        D. ensure the observance of procedural due process

  5. The above passage implies that a considerable rise in the   5.___
     quality of work of public employees can be brought about by
        A. encouraging positive employee attitudes toward work
        B. controlling personnel officers who exceed their powers
        C. creating warm personal associations among public
           employees in an agency
        D. closing loopholes in personnel organization and
           procedures

Questions 6-8.

DIRECTIONS: Questions 6 through 8 are to be answered SOLELY on
              the basis of the following passage on Employee Needs.

EMPLOYEE NEEDS

The greatest waste in industry and in government may be that of human resources. This waste usually derives not from employees' unwillingness or inability, but from management's ineptness to meet the maintenance and motivational needs of employees. Maintenance needs refer to such needs as providing employees with safe places to work, written work rules, job security, adequate salary, employer-sponsored social activities, and with knowledge of their role in the overall framework of the organization. However, of greatest significance to employees are the motivational needs of job growth, achievement, responsibility, and recognition.

Although employee dissatisfaction may stem from either poor maintenance or poor motivation factors, the outward manifestation of the dissatisfaction may be very much alike, i.e., negativism, complaints, deterioration of performance, and so forth. The improvement in the lighting of an employee's work area or raising his level of pay won't do much good if the source of the dissatisfaction is the absence of a meaningful assignment. By the same token, if an employee is dissatisfied with what he considers inequitable pay, the introduction of additional challenge in his work may simply make matters worse.

It is relatively easy for an employee to express frustration by complaining about pay, washroom conditions, fringe benefits, and so forth; but most people cannot easily express resentment in terms of the more abstract concepts concerning job growth, responsibility, and achievement.

2

It would be wrong to assume that there is no interaction between maintenance and motivational needs of employees. For example, conditions of high motivation often overshadow poor maintenance conditions. If an organization is in a period of strong growth and expansion, opportunities for job growth, responsibility, recognition, and achievement are usually abundant, but the rapid growth may have outrun the upkeep of maintenance factors. In this situation, motivation may be high, but only if employees recognize the poor maintenance conditions as unavoidable and temporary. The subordination of maintenance factors cannot go on indefinitely, even with the highest motivation.

Both maintenance and motivation factors influence the behavior of all employees, but employees are not identical and, furthermore, the needs of any individual do not remain constant. However, a broad distinction can be made between employees who have a basic orientation toward maintenance factors and those with greater sensitivity toward motivation factors.

A highly maintenance-oriented individual, preoccupied with the factors peripheral to his job rather than the job itself, is more concerned with comfort than challenge. He does not get deeply involved with his work but does with the condition of his work area, toilet facilities, and his time for going to lunch. By contrast, a strongly motivation-oriented employee is usually relatively indifferent to his surroundings and is caught up in the pursuit of work goals.

Fortunately, there are few people who are either exclusively maintenance-oriented or purely motivation-oriented. The former would be deadwood in an organization, while the latter might trample on those around him in his pursuit to achieve his goals.

6. With respect to employee motivational and maintenance needs, the management policies of an organization which is growing rapidly will PROBABLY result
    A. more in meeting motivational needs rather than maintenance needs
    B. more in meeting maintenance needs rather than motivational needs
    C. in meeting both of these needs equally
    D. in increased effort to define the motivational and maintenance needs of its employees

6.___

7. In accordance with the above passage, which of the following CANNOT be considered as an example of an employee maintenance need for railroad clerks?
    A. Providing more relief periods
    B. Providing fair salary increases at periodic intervals
    C. Increasing job responsibilities
    D. Increasing health insurance benefits

7.___

8. Most employees in an organization may be categorized as being interested in
    A. maintenance needs *only*
    B. motivational needs *only*
    C. both motivational and maintenance needs
    D. money only, to the exclusion of all other needs

8.___

Questions 9-11.

DIRECTIONS: Questions 9 through 11 are to be answered SOLELY on
the basis of the following passage on Good Employee
Practices.

GOOD EMPLOYEE PRACTICES

As a city employee, you will be expected to take an interest in
your work and perform the duties of your job to the best of your
ability and in a spirit of cooperation. Nothing shows an interest in
your work more than coming to work on time, not only at the start of
the day but also when returning from lunch. If it is necessary for
you to keep a personal appointment at lunch hour which might cause a
delay in getting back to work on time, you should explain the situation to your supervisor and get his approval to come back a little
late before you leave for lunch.

You should do everything that is asked of you willingly and
consider important even the small jobs that your supervisor gives you.
Although these jobs may seem unimportant, if you forget to do them or
if you don't do them right, trouble may develop later.

Getting along well with your fellow workers will add much to the
enjoyment of your work. You should respect your fellow workers and
try to see their side when a disagreement arises. The better you
get along with your fellow workers and your supervisor, the better you
will like your job and the better you will be able to do it.

9.   According to the above passage, in your job as a city   9.___
employee, you are expected to
A. show a willingness to cooperate on the job
B. get your supervisor's approval before keeping any
personal appointments at lunch hour
C. avoid doing small jobs that seem unimportant
D. do the easier jobs at the start of the day and the
more difficult ones later on

10. According to the above passage, getting to work on time   10.___
shows that you
A. need the job
B. have an interest in your work
C. get along well with your fellow workers
D. like your supervisor

11. According to the above passage, the one of the following   11.___
statements that is NOT true is
A. if you do a small job wrong, trouble may develop
B. you should respect your fellow workers
C. if you disagree with a fellow worker, you should try
to see his side of the story
D. the less you get along with your supervisor, the
better you will be able to do your job

4

Questions 12-15.

DIRECTIONS: Questions 12 through 15 are to be answered SOLELY on
              the basis of the following passage on Employee Suggestions.

EMPLOYEE SUGGESTIONS

To increase the effectiveness of the city government, the city
asks its employees to offer suggestions when they feel an improvement
could be made in some government operation. The Employees' Suggestions
Program was started to encourage city employees to do this. Through
this Program, which is only for city employees, cash awards may be
given to those whose suggestions are submitted and approved. Suggestions are looked for not only from supervisors but from all city
employees as any city employee may get an idea which might be approved
and contribute greatly to the solution of some problem of city government.

Therefore, all suggestions for improvement are welcome, whether
they be suggestions on how to improve working conditions, or on how
to increase the speed with which work is done, or on how to reduce or
eliminate such things as waste, time losses, accidents or fire hazards.
There are, however, a few types of suggestions for which cash awards
cannot be given. An example of this type would be a suggestion to
increase salaries or a suggestion to change the regulations about
annual leave or about sick leave. The number of suggestions sent in
has increased sharply during the past few years. It is hoped that it
will keep increasing in the future in order to meet the city's needs
for more ideas for improved ways of doing things.

12. According to the above passage, the MAIN reason why the   12.____
     city asks its employees for suggestions about government
     operations is to
         A. increase the effectiveness of the city government
         B. show that the Employees' Suggestion Program is working
            well
         C. show that everybody helps run the city government
         D. have the employee win a prize

13. According to the above passage, the Employees' Suggestion   13.____
     Program can approve awards ONLY for those suggestions that
     come from
         A. city employees
         B. city employees who are supervisors
         C. city employees who are not supervisors
         D. experienced employees of the city

14. According to the above passage, a cash award cannot be   14.____
     given through the Employees' Suggestion Program for a
     suggestion about
         A. getting work done faster
         B. helping prevent accidents on the job
         C. increasing the amount of annual leave for city employees
         D. reducing the chance of fire where city employees work

15. According to the above passage, the suggestions sent in   15.___
    during the past few years have
    A. all been approved
    B. generally been well written
    C. been mostly about reducing or eliminating waste
    D. been greater in number than before

Questions 16-18.

DIRECTIONS: Questions 16 through 18 are to be answered SOLELY on
              the basis of the following passage.

The supervisor will gain the respect of the members of his staff
and increase his influence over them by controlling his temper and
avoiding criticizing anyone publicly. When a mistake is made, the
good supervisor will talk it over with the employee quietly and privately. The supervisor will listen to the employee's story, suggest
the better way of doing the job, and offer help so the mistake won't
happen again. Before closing the discussion, the supervisor should
try to find something good to say about other parts of the employee's
work. Some praise and appreciation, along with instruction, is more
likely to encourage an employee to improve in those areas where he
is weakest.

16. A GOOD title that would show the meaning of the above   16.___
    passage would be
    A. HOW TO CORRECT EMPLOYEE ERRORS
    B. HOW TO PRAISE EMPLOYEES
    C. MISTAKES ARE PREVENTABLE
    D. THE WEAK EMPLOYEE

17. According to the above passage, the work of an employee   17.___
    who has made a mistake is more likely to improve if the
    supervisor
    A. avoids criticizing him
    B. gives him a chance to suggest a better way of doing
       the work
    C. listens to the employee's excuses to see if he is right
    D. praises good work at the same time he corrects the
       mistake

18. According to the above passage, when a supervisor needs   18.___
    to correct an employee's mistake, it is important that he
    A. allow some time to go by after the mistake is made
    B. do so when other employees are not present
    C. show his influence with his tone of voice
    D. tell other employees to avoid the same mistake

Questions 19-23.

DIRECTIONS: Questions 19 through 23 are to be answered SOLELY on
              the basis of the following passage.

In studying the relationships of people to the organizational
structure, it is absolutely necessary to identify and recognize the
informal organizational structure. These relationships are necessary

when coordination of a plan is attempted. They may be with *the boss*,
line supervisors, staff personnel, or other representatives of the
formal organization's hierarchy, and they may include the *liaison men*
who serve as the leaders of the informal organization. An acquaintanceship with the people serving in these roles in the organization,
and its formal counterpart, permits a supervisor to recognize sensi-
tive areas in which it is simple to get a conflict reaction. Avoidance
of such areas, plus conscious efforts to inform other people of his
own objectives for various plans, will usually enlist their aid and
support. Planning *without people* can lead to disaster because the
individuals who must act together to make any plan a success are more
important than the plans themselves.

19. Of the following titles, the one that MOST clearly des-   19.___
    cribes the above passage is
    A. COORDINATION OF A FUNCTION
    B. AVOIDANCE OF CONFLICT
    C. PLANNING WITH PEOPLE
    D. PLANNING OBJECTIVES

20. According to the above passage, attempts at coordinating   20.___
    plans may fail unless
    A. the plan's objectives are clearly set forth
    B. conflict between groups is resolved
    C. the plans themselves are worthwhile
    D. informal relationships are recognized

21. According to the above passage, conflict   21.___
    A. may, in some cases, be desirable to secure results
    B. produces more heat than light
    C. should be avoided at all costs
    D. possibilities can be predicted by a sensitive super-
       visor

22. The above passage implies that   22.___
    A. informal relationships are more important than formal
       structure
    B. the weakness of a formal structure depends upon
       informal relationships
    C. liaison men are the key people to consult when taking
       formal and informal structures into account
    D. individuals in a group are at least as important as
       the plans for the group

23. The above passage suggests that   23.___
    A. some planning can be disastrous
    B. certain people in sensitive areas should be avoided
    C. the supervisor should discourage acquaintanceships
       in the organization
    D. organizational relationships should be consciously
       limited

7

Questions 24-25.

DIRECTIONS: Questions 24 and 25 are to be answered SOLELY on the
              basis of the following passage.

Good personnel relations of an organization depend upon mutual
confidence, trust, and good will. The basis of confidence is understanding. Most troubles start with people who do not understand each
other. When the organization's intentions or motives are misunder-
stood, or when reasons for actions, practices, or policies are mis-
construed, complete cooperation from individuals is not forthcoming.
If management expects full cooperation from employees, it has a
responsibility of sharing with them the information which is the
foundation of proper understanding, confidence, and trust. Personnel
management has long since outgrown the days when it was the vogue to
treat them rough and tell them nothing. Up-to-date personnel management provides all possible information about the activities, aims,
and purposes of the organization. It seems altogether creditable
that a desire should exist among employees for such information which
the best-intentioned executive might think would not interest them
and which the worst-intentioned would think was none of their business.

24. The above passage implies that one of the causes of the   24.____
     difficulty which an organization might have with its
     personnel relations is that its employees
        A. have not expressed interest in the activities, aims,
           and purposes of the organization
        B. do not believe in the good faith of the organization
        C. have not been able to give full cooperation to the
           organization
        D. do not recommend improvements in the practices and
           policies of the organization

25. According to the above passage, in order for an organiza-   25.____
     tion to have good personnel relations, it is NOT essential
     that
        A. employees have confidence in the organization
        B. the purposes of the organization be understood by
           the employees
        C. employees have a desire for information about the
           organization
        D. information about the organization be communicated
           to employees

TEST 2

Questions 1-8.

DIRECTIONS: Questions 1 through 8 are to be answered SOLELY on the basis of the following passage.

Important figures in education and in public affairs have recommended development of a private organization sponsored in part by various private foundations which would offer installment payment plans to full-time matriculated students in accredited colleges and universities in the United States and Canada. Contracts would be drawn to cover either tuition and fees, or tuition, fees, room and board in college facilities, from one year up to and including six years. A special charge, which would vary with the length of the contract, would be added to the gross repayable amount. This would be in addition to interest at a rate which would vary with the income of the parents. There would be a 3% annual interest charge for families with total income, before income taxes, of $10,000 or less. The rate would increase by 1/10 of 1% for every $200 of additional net income in excess of $10,000 up to a maximum of 10% interest. Contracts would carry an insurance provision on the life of the parent or guardian who signs the contract; all contracts must have the signature of a parent or guardian. Payment would be scheduled in equal monthly installments.

1. Which of the following students would be eligible for the payment plan described in the above passage?   1.___
   A
   A. matriculated student taking six semester hours toward a graduate degree
   B. matriculated student taking seventeen semester hours toward an undergraduate degree
   C. graduate matriculated at the University of Mexico taking eighteen semester hours toward a graduate degree
   D. student taking eighteen semester hours in a special pre-matriculation program

2. According to the above passage, the organization described would be sponsored in part by   2.___
   A. private foundations
   B. colleges and universities
   C. persons in the field of education
   D. persons in public life

3. Which of the following expenses could NOT be covered by a contract with the organization described in the above passage?   3.___
   A. Tuition amounting to $4,000 per year
   B. Registration and laboratory fees
   C. Meals at restaurants near the college
   D. Rent for an apartment in a college dormitory

9

4. The total amount to be paid would include ONLY the   4.___
   A. principal
   B. principal and interest
   C. principal, interest, and special charge
   D. principal, interest, special charge, and fee

5. The contract would carry insurance on the   5.___
   A. life of the student
   B. life of the student's parents
   C. income of the parents of the student
   D. life of the parent who signed the contract

6. The interest rate for an annual loan of $5,000 from the   6.___
organization described in the above passage for a student
whose family's net income was $11,000 should be
   A. 3%   B. 3.5%   C. 4%   D. 4.5%

7. The interest rate for an annual loan of $7,000 from the   7.___
organization described in the above passage for a student
whose family's net income was $20,000 should be
   A. 5%   B. 8%   C. 9%   D. 10%

8. John Lee has submitted an application for the installment   8.___
payment plan described in the above passage. John's mother
and father have a store which grossed $100,000 last year,
but the income which the family received from the store
was $18,000 before taxes. They also had $1,000 income
from stock dividends. They paid $2,000 in income taxes.
The amount of income upon which the interest should be
based is
   A. $17,000   B. $18,000   C. $19,000   D. $21,000

Questions 9-13.

DIRECTIONS: Questions 9 through 13 are to be answered SOLELY on
the basis of the following passage.

Since an organization chart is pictorial in nature, there is a
tendency for it to be drawn in an artistically balanced and appealing
fashion, regardless of the realities of actual organizational structure. In addition to being subject to this distortion, there is the
difficulty of communicating in any organization chart the relative
importance or the relative size of various component parts of an
organizational structure. Furthermore, because of the need for sim-
plicity of design, an organization chart can never indicate the full
extent of the interrelationships among the component parts of an
organization. These interrelationships are often just as vital as the
specifications which an organization chart endeavors to indicate. Yet,
if an organization chart were to be drawn with all the wide variety of
criss-crossing communication and cooperation networks existent within
a typical organization, the chart would probably be much more confusing than informative. It is also obvious that no organization
chart as such can *prove* or *disprove* that the organizational structure
it represents is effective in realizing the objectives of the organization. At best, an organization chart can only illustrate some of
the various factors to be taken into consideration in understanding,
devising, or altering organizational arrangements.

9. According to the above passage, an organization chart can   9.___
   be expected to portray the
   A. structure of the organization along somewhat ideal lines
   B. relative size of the organizational units quite
      accurately
   C. channels of information distribution within the organi-
      zation graphically
   D. extent of the obligation of each unit to meet the
      organizational objectives

10. According to the above passage, those aspects of internal   10.___
    functioning which are NOT shown on an organization chart
    A. can be considered to have little practical application
       in the operations of the organization
    B. might well be considered to be as important as the
       structural relationships which a chart does present
    C. could be the cause of considerable confusion in the
       operations of an organization which is quite large
    D. would be most likely to provide the information
       needed to determine the overall effectiveness of an
       organization

11. In the above passage, the one of the following conditions   11.___
    which is NOT implied as being a defect of an organization
    chart is that an organization chart may
    A. present a picture of the organizational structure
       which is different from the structure that actually
       exists
    B. fail to indicate the comparative size of various
       organizational units
    C. be limited in its ability to convey some of the
       meaningful aspects of organizational relationships
    D. become less useful over a period of time during
       which the organizational facts which it illustrated
       have changed

12. The one of the following which is the MOST suitable title   12.___
    for the above passage is
    A. THE DESIGN AND CONSTRUCTION OF AN ORGANIZATION CHART
    B. THE INFORMAL ASPECTS OF AN ORGANIZATION CHART
    C. THE INHERENT DEFICIENCIES OF AN ORGANIZATION CHART
    D. THE UTILIZATION OF A TYPICAL ORGANIZATION CHART

13. It can be INFERRED from the above passage that the func-   13.___
    tion of an organization chart is to
    A. contribute to the comprehension of the organization
       form and arrangements
    B. establish the capabilities of the organization to
       operate effectively
    C. provide a balanced picture of the operations of the
       organization
    D. eliminate the need for complexity in the organization's
       structure

Questions 14-16.

DIRECTIONS: Questions 14 through 16 are to be answered SOLELY on the basis of the following passage.

In dealing with visitors to the school office, the school secretary must use initiative, tact, and good judgment. All visitors should be greeted promptly and courteously. The nature of their business should be determined quickly and handled expeditiously. Frequently, the secretary should be able to handle requests, receipts, deliveries, or passes herself. Her judgment should determine when a visitor should see members of the staff or the principal. Serious problems or doubtful cases should be referred to a supervisor.

14. In general, visitors should be handled by the   14.___
    A. school secretary   B. principal
    C. appropriate supervisor   D. person who is free

15. It is wise to obtain the following information from   15.___
    visitors:
    A. Name   B. Nature of business
    C. Address   D. Problems they have

16. All visitors who wish to see members of the staff should   16.___
    A. be permitted to do so
    B. produce identification
    C. do so for valid reasons only
    D. be processed by a supervisor

Questions 17-19.

DIRECTIONS: Questions 17 through 19 are to be answered SOLELY on the basis of the following passage.

Information regarding payroll status, salary differentials, promotional salary increments, deductions, and pension payments should be given to all members of the staff who have questions regarding these items. On occasion, if the secretary is uncertain regarding the information, the staff member should be referred to the principal or the appropriate agency. No question by a staff member regarding payroll status should be brushed aside as immaterial or irrelevant. The school secretary must always try to handle the question or pass it on to the person who can handle it.

17. If a teacher is dissatisfied with information regarding   17.___
    her salary status, as given by the school secretary, the
    matter should be
    A. dropped
    B. passed on to the principal
    C. passed on by the secretary to proper agency or the
       principal
    D. made a basis for grievance procedures

18. The following is an adequate summary of the above passage: 18.___
    A. The secretary must handle all payroll matters
    B. The secretary must handle all payroll matters or know
       who can handle them
    C. The secretary or the principal must handle all payroll
       matters
    D. Payroll matters too difficult to handle must be followed
       up until they are solved

19. The above passage implies that   19.___
    A. many teachers ask immaterial questions regarding
       payroll status
    B. few teachers ask irrelevant pension questions
    C. no teachers ask immaterial salary questions
    D. no question regarding salary should be considered
       irrelevant

Questions 20-22.

DIRECTIONS: Questions 20 through 22 are to be answered SOLELY on
              the basis of the following passage.

    The necessity for good speech on the part of the school secretary
cannot be overstated. The school secretary must deal with the general
public, the pupils, the members of the staff, and the school supervisors. In every situation which involves the general public, the
secretary serves as a representative of the school. In dealing with
pupils, the secretary's speech must serve as a model from which students
may guide themselves. Slang, colloquialisms, malapropisms, and local
dialects must be avoided.

20. The above passage implies that the speech pattern of the   20.___
    secretary must be
    A. perfect
    B. very good
    C. average
    D. on a level with that of the pupils

21. The last sentence indicates that slang   21.___
    A. is acceptable
    B. occurs in all speech
    C. might be used occasionally
    D. should be shunned

22. The above passage implies that the speech of pupils   22.___
    A. may be influenced   B. does not change readily
    C. is generally good   D. is generally poor

Questions 23-25.

DIRECTIONS: Questions 23 through 25 are to be answered SOLELY on
              the basis of the following passage.

    The school secretary who is engaged in the task of filing records
and correspondence should follow a general set of rules. Items which
are filed should be available to other secretaries or to supervisors

13

quickly and easily by means of the application of a modicum of common sense and good judgment. Items which, by their nature, may be difficult to find should be cross-indexed. Folders and drawers should be neatly and accurately labeled. There should never be a large accumulation of papers which have not been filed.

23. A good general rule to follow in filing is that materials should be   23.___
    A. placed in folders quickly
    B. neatly stored
    C. readily available
    D. cross-indexed

24. Items that are filed should be available to   24.___
    A. the secretary charged with the task of filing
    B. secretaries and supervisors
    C. school personnel
    D. the principal

25. A modicum of common sense means ____ common sense.   25.___
    A. an average amount of   B. a great deal of
    C. a little   D. no

TEST 3

Questions 1-4.

DIRECTIONS: Questions 1 through 4 are to be answered SOLELY on the basis of the following passage.

The proposition that administrative activity is essentially the same in all organizations appears to underlie some of the practices in the administration of private higher education. Although the practice is unusual in public education, there are numerous instances of industrial, governmental, or military administrators being assigned to private institutions of higher education and, to a lesser extent, of college and university presidents assuming administrative positions in other types of organizations. To test this theory that administrators are interchangeable, there is a need for systematic observation and classification. The myth that an educational administrator must first have experience in the teaching profession is firmly rooted in a long tradition that has historical prestige. The myth is bound up in the expectations of the public and personnel surrounding the administrator. Since administrative success depends significantly on how well an administrator meets the expectations others have of him, the myth may be more powerful than the special experience in helping the administrator attain organizational and educational objectives. Educational administrators who have risen through the teaching profession have often expressed nostalgia for the life of a teacher or scholar, but there is no evidence that this nostalgia contributes to administrative success.

1. Which of the following statements as completed is MOST   1.___
   consistent with the above passage?
   The greatest number of administrators has moved from
      A. industry and the military to government and universities
      B. government and universities to industry and the military
      C. government, the armed forces, and industry to colleges
         and universities
      D. colleges and universities to government, the armed
         forces, and industry

2. Of the following, the MOST reasonable inference from the   2.___
   above passage is that a specific area requiring further
   research is the
      A. place of myth in the tradition and history of the
         educational profession
      B. relative effectiveness of educational administrators
         from inside and outside the teaching profession
      C. performance of administrators in the administration
         of public colleges
      D. degree of reality behind the nostalgia for scholarly
         pursuits often expressed by educational administrators

3. According to the above passage, the value to an educational 3.___
   administrator of experience in the teaching profession
      A. lies in the firsthand knowledge he has acquired of
         immediate educational problems
      B. may lie in the belief of his colleagues, subordinates,
         and the public that such experience is necessary
      C. has been supported by evidence that the experience
         contributes to administrative success in educational
         fields
      D. would be greater if the administrator were able to
         free himself from nostalgia for his former duties

4. Of the following, the MOST suitable title for the above   4.___
   passage is
      A. EDUCATIONAL ADMINISTRATION, ITS PROBLEMS
      B. THE EXPERIENCE NEEDED FOR EDUCATIONAL ADMINISTRATION
      C. ADMINISTRATION IN HIGHER EDUCATION
      D. EVALUATING ADMINISTRATIVE EXPERIENCE

Questions 5-6.

DIRECTIONS: Questions 5 and 6 are to be answered SOLELY on the
              basis of the following passage.

   Management by objectives (MBO) may be defined as the process by
which the superior and the subordinate managers of an organization
jointly define its common goals, define each individual's major areas
of responsibility in terms of the results expected of him and use
these measures as guides for operating the unit and assessing the
contribution of each of its members.

The MBO approach requires that after organizational goals are established and communicated, targets must be set for each individual position which are congruent with organizational goals. Periodic performance reviews and a final review using the objectives set as criteria are also basic to this approach.

Recent studies have shown that MBO programs are influenced by attitudes and perceptions of the boss, the company, the reward-punishment system, and the program itself. In addition, the manner in which the MBO program is carried out can influence the success of the program. A study done in the late sixties indicates that the best results are obtained when the manager sets goals which deal with significant problem areas in the organizational unit, or with the subordinate's personal deficiencies. These goals must be clear with regard to what is expected of the subordinate. The frequency of feedback is also important in the success of a management-by-objectives program. Generally, the greater the amount of feedback, the more successful the MBO program.

5. According to the above passage, the expected output for   5.___
    individual employees should be determined
    A. after a number of reviews of work performance
    B. after common organizational goals are defined
    C. before common organizational goals are defined
    D. on the basis of an employee's personal qualities

6. According to the above passage, the management-by-   6.___
    objectives approach requires
    A. less feedback than other types of management programs
    B. little review of on-the-job performance after the
       initial setting of goals
    C. general conformance between individual goals and
       organizational goals
    D. the setting of goals which deal with minor problem
       areas in the organization

Questions 7-10.

DIRECTIONS: Questions 7 through 10 are to be answered SOLELY on
             the basis of the following passage.

Management, which is the function of executive leadership, has as its principal phases the planning, organizing, and controlling of the activities of subordinate groups in the accomplishment of organizational objectives. Planning specifies the kind and extent of the factors, forces, and effects, and the relationships among them, that will be required for satisfactory accomplishment. The nature of the objectives and their requirements must be known before determinations can be made as to what must be done, how it must be done and why, where actions should take place, who should be responsible, and similar problems pertaining to the formulation of a plan. Organizing, which creates the conditions that must be present before the execution of the plan can be undertaken successfully, cannot be done intelligently without knowledge of the organizational objectives. Control, which has to do with the constraint and regulation of activities entering into the execution of the plan, must be exercised in accordance with the characteristics and requirements of the activities demanded by the plan.

7. The one of the following which is the MOST suitable title   7.___
   for the above passage is
   A. THE NATURE OF SUCCESSFUL ORGANIZATION
   B. THE PLANNING OF MANAGEMENT FUNCTIONS
   C. THE IMPORTANCE OF ORGANIZATIONAL FUNCTIONS
   D. THE PRINCIPLE ASPECTS OF MANAGEMENT

8. It can be inferred from the above passage that the one of   8.___
   the following functions whose existence is essential to
   the existence of the other three is the
   A. regulation of the work needed to carry out a plan
   B. understanding of what the organization intends to
      accomplish
   C. securing of information of the factors necessary for
      accomplishment of objectives
   D. establishment of the conditions required for success-
      ful action

9. The one of the following which would NOT be included   9.___
   within any of the principal phases of the function of
   executive leadership as defined in the above passage is
   A. determination of manpower requirements
   B. procurement of required material
   C. establishment of organizational objectives
   D. scheduling of production

10. The conclusion which can MOST reasonably be drawn from   10.___
    the above passage is that the control phase of managing
    is most directly concerned with the
    A. influencing of policy determinations
    B. administering of suggestion systems
    C. acquisition of staff for the organization
    D. implementation of performance standards

Questions 11-12.

DIRECTIONS: Questions 11 and 12 are to be answered SOLELY on the
            basis of the following passage.

Under an open-and-above-board policy, it is to be expected that some supervisors will gloss over known shortcomings of subordinates rather than face the task of discussing them face-to-face. It is also to be expected that at least some employees whose job performance is below par will reject the supervisor's appraisal as biased and unfair. Be that as it may, these are inescapable aspects of any performance appraisal system in which human beings are involved. The supervisor who shies away from calling a spade a spade, as well as the employee with a chip on his shoulder, will each in his own way eventually be revealed in his true light -- to the benefit of the organization as a whole.

11. The BEST of the following interpretations of the above passage is that   11.___
   A. the method of rating employee performance requires immediate revision to improve employee acceptance
   B. substandard performance ratings should be discussed with employees even if satisfactory ratings are not
   C. supervisors run the risk of being called unfair by their subordinates even though their appraisals are accurate
   D. any system of employee performance rating is satisfactory if used properly

12. The BEST of the following interpretations of the above passage is that   12.___
   A. supervisors generally are not open-and-above-board with their subordinates
   B. it is necessary for supervisors to tell employees objectively how they are performing
   C. employees complain when their supervisor does not keep them informed
   D. supervisors are afraid to tell subordinates their weaknesses

Questions 13-15.

DIRECTIONS: Questions 13 through 15 are to be answered SOLELY on the basis of the following passage.

During the last decade, a great deal of interest has been generated around the phenomenon of *organizational development*, or the process of developing human resources through conscious organization effort. Organizational development (OD) stresses improving interpersonal relationships and organizational skills, such as communication, to a much greater degree than individual training ever did.

The kind of training that an organization should emphasize depends upon the present and future structure of the organization. If future organizations are to be unstable, shifting coalitions, then individual skills and abilities, particularly those emphasizing innovativeness, creativity, flexibility, and the latest technological knowledge, are crucial and individual training is most appropriate.

But if there is to be little change in organizational structure, then the main thrust of training should be group-oriented or organizational development. This approach seems better designed for overcoming hierarchical barriers, for developing a degree of interpersonal relationships which make communication along the chain of command possible, and for retaining a modicum of innovation and/or flexibility.

13. According to the above passage, group-oriented training   13.___
   is MOST useful in
   A. developing a communications system that will facilitate understanding through the chain of command
   B. highly flexible and mobile organizations

C. preventing the crossing of hierarchical barriers within an organization
D. saving energy otherwise wasted on developing methods of dealing with rigid hierarchies

14. The one of the following conclusions which can be drawn   14.___
    MOST appropriately from the above passage is that
    A. behavioral research supports the use of organizational development training methods rather than individualized training
    B. it is easier to provide individualized training in specific skills than to set up sensitivity training programs
    C. organizational development eliminates innovative or flexible activity
    D. the nature of an organization greatly influences which training methods will be most effective

15. According to the above passage, the one of the following   15.___
    which is LEAST important for large-scale organizations geared to rapid and abrupt change is
    A. current technological information
    B. development of a high degree of interpersonal relationships
    C. development of individual skills and abilities
    D. emphasis on creativity

Questions 16-18.

DIRECTIONS: Questions 16 through 18 are to be answered SOLELY on the basis of the following passage.

The increase in the extent to which each individual is personally responsible to others is most noticeable in a large bureaucracy. No one person *decides* anything; each decision of any importance is the product of an intricate process of brokerage involving individuals inside and outside the organization who feel some reason to be affected by the decision, or who have special knowledge to contribute to it. The more varied the organization's constituency, the more outside *veto-groups* will need to be taken into account. But even if no outside consultations were involved, sheer size would produce a complex process of decision. For a large organization is a deliberately created system of tensions into which each individual is expected to bring work-ways, viewpoints, and outside relationships markedly different from those of his colleagues. It is the administrator's task to draw from these disparate forces the elements of wise action from day to day, consistent with the purposes of the organization as a whole.

16. The above passage is ESSENTIALLY a description of decision-   16.___
    making as
    A. an organization process
    B. the key responsibility of the administrator
    C. the one best position among many
    D. a complex of individual decisions

19

17. Which one of the following statements BEST describes the   17.___
    responsibilities of an administrator?
    A. He modifies decisions and goals in accordance with
       pressures from within and outside the organization.
    B. He creates problem-solving mechanisms that rely on
       the varied interests of his staff and *veto-groups*.
    C. He makes determinations that will lead to attainment
       of his agency's objectives.
    D. He obtains agreement among varying viewpoints and
       interests.

18. In the context of the operations of a central public   18.___
    personnel agency, a *veto group* would LEAST likely consist
    of
    A. employee organizations
    B. professional personnel societies
    C. using agencies
    D. civil service newspapers

Questions 19-25.

DIRECTIONS: Questions 19 through 25 are to be answered SOLELY on
               the basis of the following passage, which is an extract
               from a report prepared for Department X, which outlines
               the procedure to be followed in the case of transfers
               of employees.

Every transfer, regardless of the reason therefor, requires completion of the record of transfer, Form DT 411. To denote consent to
the transfer, DT 411 should contain the signatures of the transferee
and the personnel officer(s) concerned, except that, in the case of
an involuntary transfer, the signatures of the transferee's present
and prospective supervisors shall be entered in Boxes 8A and 8B,
respectively, since the transferee does not consent. Only a permanent
employee may request a transfer; in such cases, the employee's attendance record shall be duly considered with regard to absences, late-
nesses, and accrued overtime balances. In the case of an inter-
district transfer, the employee's attendance record must be included
in Section 8A of the transfer request, Form DT 410, by the personnel
officer of the district from which the transfer is requested. The
personnel officer of the district to which the employee requested
transfer may refuse to accept accrued overtime balances in excess of
ten days.

An employee on probation shall be eligible for transfer. If such
employee is involuntarily transferred, he shall be credited for the
period of time already served on probation. However, if such transfer
is voluntary, the employee shall be required to serve the entire
period of his probation in the new position. An employee who has
occurred a disability which prevents him from performing his normal
duties may be transferred during the period of such disability to
other appropriate duties. A disability transfer requires the completion of either Form DT 414 if the disability is job-connected, or
Form DT 415 if it is not a job-connected disability. In either case,
the personnel officer of the district from which the transfer is made

20

signs in Box 6A of the first two copies and the personnel officer of
the district to which the transfer is made signs in Box 6B of the
last two copies, or, in the case of an intra-district disability
transfer, the personnel officer must sign in Box 6A of the first two
copies and Box 6B of the last two copies.

19. When a personnel officer consents to an employee's request   19.____
    for transfer from his district, this procedure requires
    that the personnel officer sign Form(s)
       A. DT 411
       B. DT 410 and DT 411
       C. DT 411 and either Form DT 414 or DT 415
       D. DT 410 and DT 411, and either Form DT 414 or DT 415

20. With respect to the time record of an employee transferred   20.____
    against his wishes during his probationary period, this
    procedure requires that
       A. he serve the entire period of his probation in his
          present office
       B. he lose his accrued overtime balance
       C. his attendance record be considered with regard to
          absences and latenesses
       D. he be given credit for the period of time he has
          already served on probation

21. Assume you are a supervisor and an employee must be trans-   21.____
    ferred into your office against his wishes.
    According to the this procedure, the box you must sign on
    the record of transfer is
       A. 6A   B. 8A   C. 6B   D. 8B

22. Under this procedure, in the case of a disability trans-   22.____
    fer, when must Box 6A on Forms DT 414 and DT 415 be signed
    by the personnel officer of the district to which the
    transfer is being made?
       A. In all cases when either Form DT 414 or Form DT 415
          is used
       B. In all cases when Form DT 414 is used and only under
          certain circumstances when Form DT 415 is used
       C. In all cases when Form DT 415 is used and only under
          certain circumstances when Form DT 414 is used
       D. Only under certain circumstances when either Form
          DT 414 or Form DT 415 is used

23. From the above passage, it may be inferred MOST correctly   23.____
    that the number of copies of Form DT 414 is
       A. no more than 2
       B. at least 3
       C. at least 5
       D. more than the number of copies of Form DT 415

24. A change in punctuation and capitalization only which   24.____
    would change one sentence into two and possibly contribute
    to somewhat greater ease of reading this report extract
    would be MOST appropriate in the
       A. 2nd sentence, 1st paragraph
       B. 3rd sentence, 1st paragraph

C. next to the last sentence, 2nd paragraph
D. 2nd sentence, 2nd paragraph

25. In the second paragraph, a word that is INCORRECTED used   25.___
    is
    A. *shall* in the 1st sentence
    B. *voluntary* in the 3rd sentence
    C. *occurred* in the 4th sentence
    D. *intra-district* in the last sentence

KEY (CORRECT ANSWERS)

TEST 1	TEST 2	TEST 3
1. D	1. B	1. C
2. C	2. A	2. B
3. D	3. C	3. B
4. B	4. C	4. B
5. A	5. D	5. B
6. A	6. B	6. C
7. C	7. B	7. D
8. C	8. C	8. B
9. A	9. A	9. C
10. B	10. B	10. D
11. D	11. D	11. C
12. A	12. C	12. B
13. A	13. A	13. A
14. C	14. A	14. D
15. D	15. B	15. B
16. A	16. C	16. A
17. D	17. C	17. C
18. B	18. B	18. B
19. C	19. D	19. A
20. D	20. B	20. D
21. D	21. D	21. D
22. D	22. A	22. D
23. A	23. C	23. B
24. B	24. B	24. B
25. C	25. C	25. C

DOCUMENTS AND FORMS

PREPARING WRITTEN MATERIALS
EXAMINATION SECTION

DIRECTIONS FOR THIS SECTION:
  Each question or incomplete statement is followed by several suggested answers or completions. Select the one that BEST answers the question or completes the statement. *PRINT THE LETTER OF THE CORRECT ANSWER IN THE SPACE AT THE RIGHT.*

TEST 1

1. Of the following types of documents, it is MOST important   1. ...
   to retain and file
   A. working drafts of reports that have been submitted in
      final form
   B. copies of letters of good will which conveyed a message
      that could not be handled by phone
   C. interoffice orders for materials which have been re-
      ceived and verified
   D. interoffice memoranda regarding the routine of stan-
      dard forms
2. The MAXIMUM number of 2 3/4" x 4 1/4" size forms which may   2. ...
   be obtained from one ream of 17" x 22" paper is
   A. 4,000   B. 8,000   C. 12,000   D. 16,000
3. On a general organization chart, staff positions NORMALLY   3. ...
   should be pictured
   A. directly above the line positions to which they report
   B. to the sides of the main flow lines
   C. within the box of the highest level subordinate posi-
      tions pictured
   D. directly below the line positions which report to them
4. When an administrator is diagramming an office layout, of   4. ...
   the following, his PRIMARY job *generally* should be to indicate the
   A. lighting intensities that will be required by each
      operator
   B. noise level that will be produced by the various equip-
      ment employed in the office
   C. direction of the work flow and the distance involved in
      each transfer
   D. durability of major pieces of office equipment current-
      ly in use or to be utilized
5. One common guideline or rule-of-thumb ratio for evaluating   5. ...
   the efficiency of files is the number of records requested
   divided by the number of records filed. *Generally*, if this
   ratio is very low, it would point MOST directly to the need
   for
   A. improving the indexing and coding systems
   B. improving the charge-out procedures
   C. exploring the need for transferring records from active
      storage to the archives
   D. exploring the need to encourage employees to keep more
      records in their private files
6. The GREATEST percentage of money spent on preparing and   6. ...
   keeping the usual records in an office *generally* is ex-
   pended for which of the following?
   A. Renting space in which to place the record-keeping
      equipment
   B. Paying salaries of record-preparing and record-keep-
      ing personnel

1

    C. Depreciation of purchased record-preparation and re-
       cord-keeping machines
    D. Paper and forms upon which to place the records

7. In a certain office, file folders are constantly being   7. ...
removed from the files for use by administrators. At the
same time, new material is coming in to be filed in some
of these folders.
Of the following, the BEST way to avoid delays in filing
of the new material and to keep track of the removed folders is to

    A. keep a sheet listing all folders removed from the file,
       who has them, and a follow-up date to check on their
       return; attach to this list new material received for
       filing
    B. put an "out" slip in the place of any file folder re-
       moved, telling what folder is missing, date removed,
       and who has it; file new material received at front
       of files
    C. put a temporary "out" folder in place of the one re-
       moved, giving title or subject, date removed, and who
       has it; put into this temporary folder any new material
       received
    D. keep a list of all folders removed and who has them;
       forward any new material received for filing while a
       folder is out to the person who has it

8. Folders labeled "Miscellaneous" should be used in an al-   8. ...
phabetic filing system MAINLY to
    A. provide quick access to recent material
    B. avoid setting up individual folders for infrequent
       correspondence
    C. provide temporary storage for less important documents
    D. temporarily hold papers which will not fit into already
       crowded individual folders

9. Out-of-date and seldom-used records should be removed pe-   9. ...
riodically from the files because
    A. overall responsibility for records will be transferred
       to the person in charge of the central storage files
    B. duplicate copies of every record are not needed
    C. valuable filing space will be regained and the time
       needed to find a current record will be cut down
    D. worthwhile suggestions on improving the filing system
       will result whenever this is done

10. Of the following, the BEST reason for discarding certain   10. ...
material from office files would be that the
    A. files are crowded   B. material in the files is old
    C. material duplicates information obtainable from other
       sources in the files
    D. material is referred to most often by employees in an
       adjoining office

11. Of the following, the MAIN factor contributing to the ex-   11. ...
pense of maintaining an office procedure manual would be the
    A. infrequent use of the manual
    B. need to revise it regularly
    C. cost of loose-leaf binders   D. high cost of printing

12. The suggestion that memos or directives which circulate   12. ...
among subordinates be initialed by each employee is a

2

A. *poor one,* because, with modern copying machines, it would be possible to supply every subordinate with a copy of each message for his personal use

B. *good one,* because it relieves the supervisor of blame for the action of subordinates who have read and initialed the messages

C. *poor one,* because initialing the memo or directive is no guarantee that the subordinate has read the material

D. *good one,* because it can be used as a record by the supervisor to show that his subordinates have received the message and were responsible for reading it

13. Of the following, the MOST important reason for micro-filming office records is to   13. ...
    A. save storage space needed to keep records
    B. make it easier to get records when needed
    C. speed up the classification of information
    D. shorten the time which records must be kept

14. Your office filing cabinets have become so overcrowded   14. ...
that it is difficult to use the files.
Of the following, the *most* desirable step for you to take
FIRST to relieve this situation would be to
    A. assign your assistant to spend some time each day reviewing the material in the files and to give you his recommendations as to what material may be discarded
    B. discard all material which has been in the files more than a given number of years
    C. submit a request for additional filing cabinets in your next budget request
    D. transfer enough material to the central storage room of your agency to give you the amount of additional filing space needed

15. In indexing names of business firms and other organiza-   15. ...
tions, one of the rules to be followed is:
    A. The word "and" is considered an indexing unit.
    B. When a firm name includes the full name of a person who is not well known, the person's first name is considered as the first indexing unit.
    C. Usually, the units in a firm name are indexed in the order in which they are written.
    D. When a firm's name is made up of single letters (such as ABC Corp.), the letters taken together are considered as more than one indexing unit.

16. Assume that your unit processes confidential forms which   16. ...
are submitted by persons seeking financial assistance. An individual comes to your office, gives you his name, and states that he would like to look over a form which he sent in about a week ago because he believes he omitted some important information.
Of the following, the BEST thing for you to do *first* is to
    A. locate the proper form
    B. call the individual's home telephone number to verify his identity
    C. ask the individual if he has proof of his identity
    D. call the security office

17. An employee has been assigned to open her division head's   17. ...
mail and place it on his desk. One day, the employee opens

a letter which she then notices is marked "Personal."
Of the following, the BEST action for her to take is to
    A. write "Personal" on the letter and staple the envelope
       to the back of the letter
    B. ignore the matter and treat the letter the same way
       as the others
    C. give it to another division head to hold until her own
       division head comes into the office
    D. leave the letter in the envelope and write "Sorry -
       opened by mistake" on the envelope, and initial it

18. The MOST important reason for having a filing system is to 18. ...
    A. get papers out of the way
    B. have a record of everything that has happened
    C. retain information to justify your actions
    D. enable rapid retrieval of information

19. The system of filing which is used MOST frequently is   19. ...
   called
    A. alphabetic filing   B. alphanumeric filing
    C. geographic filing   D. numeric filing

20. In judging the adequacy of a standard office form, which 20. ...
   of the following is LEAST important?
    A. Date of the form   B. Legibility of the form
    C. Size of the form   D. Design of the form

21. Assume tha tthe letters and reports which are dictated 21. ...
   to you fall into a few distinct subject-matter areas.
   The practice of trying to familiarize yourself with the
   terminology in these areas is
    A. *good,* because you will have a basis for commenting
       on the dictated material
    B. *good,* because it will be easier to take the dictation
       at the rate at which it is given
    C. *poor,* because the functions and policies of an office
       are not of your concern
    D. *poor,* because it will take too much time away from
       your assigned work

22. A letter was dictated on June 9, 1985 and was ready to be 22. ...
   typed on June 12. The letter was typed on June 13, signed
   on June 14, and mailed on June 14. The date that, *ordinarily,* should have appeared on the letter is
    A. June 9, 1985   B. June 12, 1985
    C. June 13,1985   D. June 14, 1985

23. Of the following, the BEST reason for putting the "key   23. ...
   point" at the beginning of a letter is that it
    A. may save time for the reader
    B. is standard practice in writing letters
    C. will more likely be typed correctly
    D. cannot logically be placed elsewhere

24. As a supervisor, you have been asked to attend committee 24. ...
   meetings and take the minutes.
   The body of such minutes, *generally,* consists of
    A. the date and place of the meeting and the list of per-
       sons present
    B. an exact verbatim report of everything that was said by
       each person who spoke
    C. a clear description of each matter discussed and the
       action decided on

D. the agenda of the meeting

25. When typing a rough draft from a transcribing machine, a   25. ...
stenographer under your supervision reaches a spot on the
tape that is virtually inaudible.
Of the following, the MOST advisable action that you should
recommend to her is to
    A. guess what the dictator intended to say based on what
       he said in the parts that are clear
    B. ask the dictator to listen to his unsatisfactory dicta-
       tion
    C. leave an appropriate amount of space for that portion
       that is inaudible
    D. stop typing the draft and send a note to the dictator
       identifying the item that could not be completed

TEST 2

1. To tell a newly employed clerk to fill a top drawer of a   1. ...
four-drawer cabinet with heavy folders which will be often
used and to keep lower drawers only partly filled, is
    A. *good*, because a tall person would have to bend un-
       necessarily if he had to use a lower drawer
    B. *bad*, because the file cabinet may tip over when the
       top drawer is opened
    C. *good*, because it is the most easily reachable drawer
       for the average person
    D. *bad*, because a person bending down at another drawer
       may accidentally bang his head on the bottom of the
       drawer when he straightens up

2. If you have requisitioned a "ream" of paper in order to   2. ...
duplicate a single page office announcement, how many announcements can be printed from the one package of paper?
    A. 200   B. 500   C. 700   D. 1,000

3. In the operations of a government agency, a voucher is   3. ...
ORDINARILY used to
    A. refer someone to the agency for a position or assignment
    B. certify that an agency's records of financial transac-
       tions are accurate
    C. order payment from agency funds of a stated amount to
       an individual
    D. enter a statement of official opinion in the records
       of the agency

4. Of the following types of cards used in filing systems, the 4. ...
one which is generally MOST helpful in locating records
which might be filed under more than one subject is the
    A. out card   B. tickler card
    C. cross-reference card D. visible index card

5. The type of filing system in which one does NOT need to   5. ...
refer to a card index in order to find the folder is called
    A. alphabetic   B. geographic
    C. subject   D. locational

6. Of the following, records management is LEAST concerned   6. ...
with
    A. the development of the best method for retrieving
       important information

5

      B. deciding what records should be kept
      C. deciding the number of appointments a client will need
      D. determining the types of folders to be used

7. If records are continually removed from a set of files   7. ...
   without "charging" them to the borrower, the filing system
   will soon become ineffective.
   Of the following terms, the one which is NOT applied to a
   form used in the charge-out system is a
      A. requisition card   B. out-folder
      C. record retrieval form   D. substitution card

8. A new clerk has been told to put 500 cards in alphabetical   8. ...
   order. Another clerk suggests that she divide the cards
   into four groups such as A to F, G to L, M to R, and S to
   Z, and then alphabetize these four smaller groups. The
   suggested method is
      A. *poor*, because the clerk will have to handle the
         sheets more than once and will waste time
      B. *good*, because it saves time, is more accurate, and
         is less tiring
      C. *good*, because she will not have to concentrate on
         it so much when it is in smaller groups
      D. *poor*, because this method is much more tiring than
         straight alphabetizing

9. Of the following duplicating machines, the one which re-   9. ...
   quires the use of a stencil is the
      A. photostat B. xerograph C. mimeograph D. thermofax

10. Suppose a clerk has been given pads of pre-printed forms   10. ...
    to use when taking phone messages for others in her office.
    The clerk is then observed using scraps of paper and not
    the forms for writing her messages.
    It should be explained that the BEST reason for using the
    forms is that
       A. they act as a check list to make sure that the impor-
          tant information is taken
       B. she is expected to do her work in the same way as
          others in the office
       C. they make sure that unassigned paper is not wasted
          on phone messages
       D. learning to use these forms will help train her to
          use more difficult forms

11. The high speed duplication process used for producing   11. ...
    large quantities of SUPERIOR quality copy of 4,000 to
    8,000 copies per hour is called
       A. photocopying   B. offset duplicating
       C. spirit duplicating   D. mimeographing

12. Of the following, the MAIN reason a stock clerk keeps a   12. ...
    perpetual inventory of supplies in the storeroom is that
    such an inventory will
       A. eliminate the need for a physical inventory
       B. provide a continuous record of supplies on hand
       C. indicate whether a shipment of supplies is satisfactory
       D. dictate the terms of the purchase order

13. As a supervisor, you may be required to handle different   13. ...
    types of correspondence.
    Of the following types of letters, it would be MOST impor-
    tant to promptly seal which kind of letter?

6

    A. One marked "confidential" B. Those containing enclosures
    C. Any letter to be sent airmail
    D. Those in which carbons will be sent along with the
       original

14. While opening incoming mail, you notice that one letter   14. ...
    indicates that an enclosure was to be included but, even
    after careful inspection, you are not able to find the in-
    formation to which this refers.
    Of the following, the thing that you should do FIRST is
    A. replace the letter in its envelope and return it to
       the sender
    B. file the letter until the sender's office mails the
       missing information
    C. type out a letter to the sender informing him of his
       error
    D. make a notation in the margin of the letter that the
       enclosure was omitted

15. You have been given a check list and assigned the respon-   15. ...
    sibility of inspecting certain equipment in the various
    offices of your agency.
    Which of the following is the GREATEST advantage of the
    check list?
    A. It indicates which equipment is in greatest demand.
    B. Each piece of equipment on the check list will be
       checked only once.
    C. It helps to insure that the equipment listed will
       not be overlooked.
    D. The equipment listed suggests other equipment you
       should look for.

16. The BEST way to evaluate the overall state of completion   16. ...
    of a construction project is to check the progress estimate
    against the
    A. inspection work sheet   B. construction schedule
    C. inspector's check list
    D. equipment maintenance schedule

17. The usual contract for agency work includes a section en-   17. ...
    titled, "Instructions to Bidders," which states that the
    A. contractor agrees that he has made his own examina-
       tion and will make no claim for damages on account
       of errors or omissions
    B. contractor shall not make claims for damages of any
       discrepancy, error or omission in any plans
    C. estimates of quantities and calculations are guaran-
       teed by the agency to be correct and are deemed to be
       a representation of the conditions affecting the work
    D. plans, measurements, dimensions and conditions under
       which the work is to be performed are guaranteed by
       the agency

18. In order to avoid disputes over payments for extra work   18. ...
    in a contract for construction, the BEST procedure to
    follow would be to
    A. have contractor submit work progress reports daily
    B. insert a special clause in the contract specifications
    C. have a representative on the job at all times to verify
       conditions
    D. allocate a certain percentage of the cost of the job to
       cover such expenses

19. Prior to the installation of equipment called for in the   19. ...
    specifications, the contractor is USUALLY required to
    submit for approval
    A. sets of shop drawings
    B. a set of revised specifications
    C. a detailed description of the methods of work to be
       used
    D. a complete list of skilled and unskilled tradesmen he
       proposes to use
20. During the actual construction work, the CHIEF value of a 20. ...
    construction schedule is to
    A. insure that the work will be done on time
    B. reveal whether production is falling behind
    C. show how much equipment and material is required for
       the project
    D. furnish data as to the methods and techniques of con-
       struction operations

KEY (CORRECT ANSWERS)

TEST 1

1.	D		11.	B
2.	D		12.	D
3.	B		13.	A
4.	C		14.	A
5.	C		15.	C
6.	B		16.	C
7.	C		17.	D
8.	B		18.	D
9.	C		19.	A
10.	C		20.	A

21.	B
22.	D
23.	A
24.	C
25.	C

TEST 2

1.	B		11.	B
2.	B		12.	B
3.	C		13.	A
4.	C		14.	D
5.	A		15.	C
6.	C		16.	B
7.	C		17.	A
8.	B		18.	C
9.	C		19.	A
10.	A		20.	B

RECORD KEEPING
EXAMINATION SECTION
TEST 1

DIRECTIONS: Each question or incomplete statement is followed by several suggested answers or completions. Select the one that BEST answers the question or completes the statement. *PRINT THE LETTER OF THE CORRECT ANSWER IN THE SPACE AT THE RIGHT.*

Questions 1-15.

DIRECTIONS: Questions 1 through 15 are to be answered on the basis of the following list of company names below. Arrange a file alphabetically, word-by-word, disregarding punctuation, conjunctions, and apostrophes. Then answer the questions.

A Bee C Reading Materials
ABCO Parts
A Better Course for Test Preparation
AAA Auto Parts Co.
A-Z Auto Parts, Inc.
Aabar Books
Abbey, Joanne
Boman-Sylvan Law Firm
BMW Autowerks
C Q Service Company
Chappell-Murray, Inc.
E&E Life Insurance
Emcrisco
Gigi Arts
Gordon, Jon & Associates
SOS Plumbing
Schmidt, J.B. Co.

1. Which of these files should appear FIRST?   1.___
   A. ABCO Parts
   B. A Bee C Reading Materials
   C. A Better Course for Test Preparation
   D. AAA Auto Parts Co.

2. Which of these files should appear SECOND?   2.___
   A. A-Z Auto Parts, Inc.
   B. A Bee C Reading Materials
   C. A Better Course for Test Preparation
   D. AAA Auto Parts Co.

3. Which of these files should appear THIRD?   3.___
   A. ABCO Parts
   B. A Bee C Reading Materials
   C. Aabar Books
   D. AAA Auto Parts Co.

4. Which of these files should appear FOURTH?   4.___
   A. ABCO Parts
   B. A Bee C Reading Materials
   C. Abbey, Joanne
   D. AAA Auto Parts Co.

5. Which of these files should appear LAST?   5.___
   A. Gordon, Jon & Associates
   B. Gigi Arts
   C. Schmidt, J.B. Co.
   D. SOS Plumbing

6. Which of these files should appear between A-Z Auto Parts,   6.___
   Inc. and Abbey, Joanne?
   A. A Bee C Reading Materials
   B. AAA Auto Parts Co.
   C. Aabar Books
   D. A Better Course for Test Preparation

7. Which of these files should appear between ABCO Parts and   7.___
   Aabar Books?
   A. A Bee C Reading Materials
   B. Abbey, Joanne
   C. Aabar Books
   D. A-Z Auto Parts

8. Which of these files should appear between Abbey, Joanne   8.___
   and Boman-Sylvan Law Firm?
   A. A Better Course for Test Preparation
   B. BMW Autowerks
   C. A-Z Auto Parts,Inc.
   D. Aabar Books

9. Which of these files should appear between Abbey, Joanne   9.___
   and C Q Service?
   A. A-Z Auto Parts,Inc.   B. BMW Autowerks
   C. Choices A and B   D. Chappell-Murray, Inc.

10. Which of these files should appear between C Q Service   10.___
    Company and Emcrisco?
    A. Chappell-Murray,Inc.   B. E&E Life Insurance
    C. Gigi Arts   D. Choices A and B

11. Which of these files should NOT appear between C Q Service   11.___
    Company and E&E Life Insurance?
    A. Gordon, Jon & Associates
    B. Emcrisco
    C. Gigi Arts
    D. All of the above

12. Which of these files should appear between Chappell-Murray   12.___
    Inc.,   and Gigi Arts?
    A. CQ Service Inc.   E&E Life Insurance, and Emcrisco
    B. Emcrisco, E&E Life Insurance, and Gordon, Jon &
       Associates

C. E&E Life Insurance and Emcrisco
D. Emcrisco and Gordon, Jon & Associates

13. Which of these files should appear between Gordon, Jon &   13.___
    Associates and SOS Plumbing?
       A. Gigi Arts   B. Schmidt, J.B. Co.
       C. Choices A and B   D. None of the above

14. Ea ch of the choices lists the four files in their proper   14.___
    alphabetical order except
       A. E&E Life Insurance; Gigi Arts; Gordon, Jon & Associ-
          ates; SOS Plumbing
       B. E&E Life Insurance; Emcrisco; Gigi Arts; SOS Plumbing
       C. Emcrisco; Gordon, Jon & Associates; Schmidt, J.B. Co.;
          SOS Plumbing
       D. Emcrisco; Gigi Arts; Gordon, Jon & Associates; SOS
          Plumbing

15. Which of the choices lists the four files in their proper   15.___
    alphabetical order?
       A. Gigi Arts; Gordon, Jon & Associates; SOS Plumbing;
          Schmidt, J.B. Co.
       B. Gordon, Jon & Associates; Gigi Arts; Schmidt, J.B.
          Co.; SOS Plumbing
       C. Gordon, Jon & Associates; Gigi Arts; SOS Plumbing;
          Schmidt, J.B. Co.
       D. Gigi Arts; Gordon, Jon & Associates; Schmidt, J.B.
          Co.; SOS Plumbing

16. The alphabetical filing order of two businesses with   16.___
    identical names is determined by the
       A. length of time each business has been operating
       B. addresses of the businesses
       C. last name of the company president
       D. none of the above

17. In an alphabetical filing system, if a business name   17.___
    includes a number, it should be
       A. disregarded
       B. considered a number and placed at the end of an
          alphabetical section
       C. treated as though it were written in words and alpha-
          betized accordingly
       D. considered a number and placed at the beginning of
          an alphabetical section

18. If a business name includes a contraction (such as *don't*   18.___
    or *it's*), how should that word be treated in an alpha-
    betical filing system?
       A. Divide the word into its separate parts and treat it
          as two words.
       B. Ignore the letters that come after the apostrophe.
       C. Ignore the word that contains the contraction.
       D. Ignore the apostrophe and consider all letters in
          the contraction.

19. In what order should the parts of an address be considered   19.___
    when using an alphabetical filing system?
       A. City or town; state; street name; house or building
          number
       B. State; city or town; street name; house or building
          number
       C. House or building number; street name; city or town;
          state
       D. Street name; city or town; state

20. A business record should be cross-referenced when a(n)   20.___
       A. organization is known by an abbreviated name
       B. business has a name change because of a sale, incor-
          poration, or other reason
       C. business is known by a *coined* or common name which
          differs from a dictionary spelling
       D. all of the above

21. A geographical filing system is MOST effective when   21.___
       A. location is more important than name
       B. many names or titles sound alike
       C. dealing with companies who have offices all over the
          world
       D. filing personal and business files

Questions 22-25.

DIRECTIONS: Questions 22 through 25 are to be answered on the
              basis of the list of items below, which are to be
              filed geographically. Organize the items geographically
              and then answer the questions.

              1. University Press at Berkeley, U.S.
              2. Maria Sanchez, Mexico City, Mexico
              3. Great Expectations Ltd. in London, England
              4. Justice League, Cape Town, South Africa, Africa
              5. Crown Pearls Ltd. in London, England
              6. Joseph Prasad in London, England

22. Which of the following arrangements of the items is   22.___
    composed according to the policy of: *Continent, Country,
    City, Firm or Individual Name*?
       A. 5, 3, 4, 6, 2, 1   B. 4, 5, 3, 6, 2, 1
       C. 1, 4, 5, 3, 6, 2   D. 4, 5, 3, 6, 1, 2

23. Which of the following files is arranged according to   23.___
    the policy of: *Continent, Country, City, Firm or
    Individual Name*?
       A. South Africa. Africa. Cape Town. Justice League
       B. Mexico. Mexico City. Maria Sanchez
       C. North America. United States. Berkeley. University
          Press
       D. England. Europe. London. Prasad, Joseph

24. Which of the following arrangements of the items is composed according to the policy of: *Country, City, Firm or Individual Name*?

    A. 5, 6, 3, 2, 4, 1   B. 1, 5, 6, 3, 2, 4

    C. 6, 5, 3, 2, 4, 1   D. 5, 3, 6, 2, 4, 1

24.____

25. Which of the following files is arranged according to a policy of: *Country, City, Firm or Individual Name*?

    A. England. London. Crown Pearls Ltd.

    B. North America. United States. Berkeley. University Press

    C. Africa. Cape Town. Justice League

    D. Mexico City. Mexico. Maria Sanchez

25.____

26. Under which of the following circumstances would a phonetic filing system be MOST effective?

    A. When the person in charge of filing can't spell very well

    B. With large files with names that sound alike

    C. With large files with names that are spelled alike

    D. All of the above

26.____

Questions 27-29.

DIRECTIONS: Questions 27 through 29 are to be answered on the basis of the following list of numerical files.

    1. 391-023-100
    2. 361-132-170
    3. 385-732-200
    4. 381-432-150
    5. 391-632-387
    6. 361-423-303
    7. 391-123-271

27. Which of the following arrangements of the files follows a consecutive-digit system?

    A. 2, 3, 4, 1   B. 1, 5, 7, 3

    C. 2, 4, 3, 1   D. 3, 1, 5, 7

27.____

28. Which of the following arrangements follows a terminal-digit system?

    A. 1, 7, 2, 4, 3   B. 2, 1, 4, 5, 7

    C. 7, 6, 5, 4, 3   D. 1, 4, 2, 3, 7

28.____

29. Which of the following lists follows a middle-digit system?

    A. 1, 7, 2, 6, 4, 5, 3   B. 1, 2, 7, 4, 6, 5, 3

    C. 7, 2, 1, 3, 5, 6, 4   D. 7, 1, 2, 4, 6, 5, 3

29.____

Questions 30-31.

DIRECTIONS: Questions 30 and 31 are to be answered on the basis
of the following information.

1. Reconfirm Laura Bates appointment with James Caldecort
on December 12 at 9:30 A.M.
2. Laurence Kinder contact Julia Lucas on August 3 and set
up a meeting for week of September 23 at 4 P.M.
3. John Lutz contact Larry Waverly on August 3 and set up
appointment for September 23 at 9:30 A.M.
4. Call for tickets for Gerry Stanton August 21 for New
Jersey on September 23, flight 143 at 4:43 P.M.

30. A chronological file for the above information would be   30.___
A. 4, 3, 2, 1   B. 3, 2, 4, 1
C. 4, 2, 3, 1   D. 3, 1, 2, 4

31. Using the above information, a chronological file for the   31.___
date of September 23 would be
A. 2, 3, 4   B. 3, 1, 4   C. 3, 2, 4   D. 4, 3, 2

Questions 32-34.

DIRECTIONS: Questions 32 through 34 are to be answered on the
basis of the following information.

1. Call Roger Epstein, Ashoke Naipaul, Jon Anderson, and
Sarah Washington on April 19 at 1:00 P.M. to set up
meeting with Alika D'Ornay for June 6 in New York.
2. Call Martin Ames before noon on April 19 to confirm
afternoon meeting with Bob Greenwood on April 20th.
3. Set up meeting room at noon for 2:30 P.M. meeting on
April 19th
4. Ashley Stanton contact Bob Greenwood at 9:00 A.M. on
April 20 and set up meeting for June 6 at 8:30 A.M.
5. Carol Guiland contact Shelby Van Ness during afternoon
of April 20 and set up meeting for June 6 at 10:00 A.M.
6. Call airline and reserve tickets on June 6 for
Roger Epstein trip to Denver on July 8
7. Meeting at 2:30 P.M. on April 19th

32. A chronological file for all of the above information   32.___
would be
A. 2, 1, 3, 7, 5, 4, 6   B. 3, 7, 2, 1, 4, 5, 6
C. 3, 7, 1, 2, 5, 4, 6   D. 2, 3, 1, 7, 4, 5, 6

33. A chronological file for the date of April 19th would be   33.___
A. 2, 3, 7, 1   B. 2, 3, 1, 7
C. 7, 1, 3, 2   D. 3, 7, 1, 2

34. Add the following information to the file, and then   34.___
    create a chronological file for April 20th:
    8. April 20: 3:00 P.M. meeting between Bob Greenwood
    and Martin Ames.
        A. 4, 5, 8   B. 4, 8, 5   C. 8, 5, 4   D. 5, 4, 8

35. The PRIMARY advantage of computer records filing over   35.___
    a manual system is
        A. speed of retrieval   B. accuracy
        C. cost   D. potential file loss

———

KEY (CORRECT ANSWERS)

1. B	11. D	21. A	31. C
2. C	12. C	22. B	32. D
3. D	13. D	23. C	33. B
4. A	14. C	24. D	34. A
5. C	15. A	25. A	35. A
6. C	16. B	26. B	
7. D	17. C	27. C	
8. B	18. D	28. D	
9. B	19. A	29. A	
10. D	20. D	30. B	

———

PREPARING WRITTEN MATERIAL

PARAGRAPH REARRANGEMENT

COMMENTARY

The sentences which follow are in scrambled order. You are to rearrange them in proper order and indicate the letter choice containing the correct answer at the space at the right.

Each group of sentences in this section is actually a paragraph presented in scrambled order. Each sentence in the group has a place in that paragraph; no sentence is to be left out. You are to read each group of sentences and decide upon the best order in which to put the sentences so as to form as well-organized paragraph.

The questions in this section measure the ability to solve a problem when all the facts relevant to its solution are not given.

More specifically, certain positions of responsibility and authority require the employee to discover connections between events sometimes, apparently, unrelated. In order to do this, the employee will find it necessary to correctly infer that unspecified events have probably occurred or are likely to occur. This ability becomes especially important when action must be taken on incomplete information.

Accordingly, these questions require competitors to choose among several suggested alternatives, each of which presents a different sequential arrangement of the events. Competitors must choose the MOST logical of the suggested sequences.

In order to do so, they may be required to draw on general knowledge to infer missing concepts or events that are essential to sequencing the given events. Competitors should be careful to infer only what is essential to the sequence. The plausibility of the wrong alternatives will always require the inclusion of unlikely events or of additional chains of events which are NOT essential to sequencing the given events.

It's very important to remember that you are looking for the best of the four possible choices, and that the best choice of all may not even be one of the answers you're given to choose from.

There is no one right way to these problems. Many people have found it helpful to first write out the order of the sentences, as they would have arranged them, on their scrap paper before looking at the possible answers. If their optimum answer is there, this can save them some time. If it isn't, this method can still give insight into solving the problem. Others find it most helpful to just go through each of the possible choices, contrasting each as they go along. You should use whatever method feels comfortable, and works, for you.

While most of these types of questions are not that difficult, we've added a higher percentage of the difficult type, just to give you more practice. Usually there are only one or two questions on this section that contain such subtle distinctions that you're unable to answer confidently, and you then may find yourself stuck deciding between two possible choices, neither of which you're sure about.

———

EXAMINATION SECTION
Preparing Written Material

Directions: The following groups of sentences need to be arranged in an order that makes sense. Select the letter preceding the sequence that represents the best sentence order. *PRINT THE LETTER OF THE CORRECT ANSWER IN THE SPACE AT THE RIGHT.*

Group 1

1. _____

1)   The ostrich egg shell's legendary toughness makes it an excellent substitute for certain types of dishes or dinnerware, and in parts of Africa ostrich shells are cut and decorated for use as containers for water.

2)   Since prehistoric times, people have used the enormous egg of the ostrich as a part of their diet, a practice which has required much patience and hard work—to hard-boil an ostrich egg takes about four hours.

3)   Opening the egg's shell, which is rock hard and nearly an inch thick, requires heavy tools, such as a saw or chisel; from inside, a baby ostrich must use a hornlike projection on its beak as a miniature pick-axe to escape from the egg.

4)   The offspring of all higher-order animals originate from single egg cells that are carried by mothers, and most of these eggs are relatively small, often microscopic.

5)   The egg of the African ostrich, however, weighs a massive thirty pounds, making it the largest single cell on earth, and a common object of human curiosity and wonder.

The best order is

A.   5 4 1 2 3
B.   1 4 5 3 2
C.   4 2 3 5 1
D.   4 5 2 3 1

Group 2

1)   Typically only a few feet high on the open sea, individual tsunami have been known to circle the entire globe two or three times if their progress is not interrupted, but are not usually dangerous until they approach the shallow water that surrounds land masses.

2)   Some of the most terrifying and damaging hazards caused by earth-quakes are tsunami, which were once called "tidal waves"—a poorly chosen name, since these waves have nothing to do with tides.

3)   Then a wave, slowed by the sudden drag on the lower part of its moving water column, will pile upon itself, sometimes reaching a height of over 100 feet.

4)   Tsunami (Japanese for "great harbor wave") are seismic waves that are caused by earthquakes near oceanic trenches, and once triggered, can travel up to 600 miles an hour on the open ocean.

5)   A land-shoaling tsunami is capable of extraordinary destruction; some tsunami have deposited large boats miles inland, washed out two-foot-thick seawalls, and scattered locomotive trains over long distances.

The best order is

A.   4 1 3 2 5
B.   1 3 4 2 5
C.   5 1 3 2 4
D.   2 4 1 3 5

Group 3

1) Soon, by the 1940's, jazz was the most popular type of music among American intellectuals and college students.

2) In the early days of jazz, it was considered "lowdown" music, or music that was played only in rough, disreputable bars and taverns.

3) However, jazz didn't take long to develop from early ragtime melodies into more complex, sophisticated forms, such as Charlie Parker's "bebop" style of jazz.

4) After charismatic band leaders such as Duke Ellington and Count Basie brought jazz to a larger audience, and jazz continued to evolve into more complicated forms, white audiences began to accept and even to enjoy the new American art form.

5) Many white Americans, who then dictated the tastes of society, were wary of music that was played almost exclusively in black clubs in the poorer sections of cities and towns.

The best order is

A.   5 4 3 2 1
B.   2 5 3 4 1
C.   4 5 3 1 2
D.   1 2 4 3 5

Group 4

1)   Then, hanging in a windless place, the magnetized end of the needle would always point to the south.

2)   The needle could then be balanced on the rim of a cup, or the edge of a fingernail, but this balancing act was hard to maintain, and the needle often fell off.

3)   Other needles would point to the north, and it was important for any traveler finding his way with a compass to remember which kind of magnetized needle he was carrying.

4)   To make some of the earliest compasses in recorded history, ancient Chinese "magicians" would rub a needle with a piece of magnetized iron called a lodestone.

5)   A more effective method of keeping the needle free to swing with its magnetic pull was to attach a strand of silk to the center of the needle with a tiny piece of wax.

The best order is

A.   4 2 5 1 3
B.   4 3 5 2 1
C.   4 5 2 1 3
D.   4 1 3 5 2

Group 5

1)   The now-famous first mate of the *HMS Bounty*, Fletcher Christian, founded one of the world's most peculiar civilizations in 1790.

2)   The men knew they had just committed a crime for which they could be hanged, so they set sail for Pitcairn, a remote, abandoned island in the far eastern region of the Polynesian archipelago, accompanied by twelve Polynesian women and six men.

3)   In a mutiny that has become legendary, Christian and the others forced Captain Bligh into a lifeboat and set him adrift off the coast of Tonga in April of 1789.

4)   In early 1790, the *Bounty* landed at Pitcairn Island, where the men lived out the rest of their lives and founded an isolated community which to this day includes direct descendants of Christian and the other crewmen.

5)   The *Bounty*, commanded by Captain William Bligh, was in the middle of a global voyage, and Christian and his shipmates had come to the conclusion that Bligh was a reckless madman who would lead them to their deaths unless they took the ship from him.

The best order is

A.   4 5 3 2 1
B.   1 3 5 2 4
C.   1 5 3 2 4
D.   3 1 5 4 2

Group 6

1) But once the vines had been led to make orchids, the flowers had to be carefully hand-pollinated, because unpollinated orchids usually lasted less than a day, wilting and dropping off the vine before it had even become dark.

2) The Totonac farmers discovered that looping a vine back around once it reached a five-foot height on its host tree would cause the vine to flower.

3) Though they knew how to process the fruit pods and extract vanilla's flavoring agent, the Totonacs also knew that a wild vanilla vine did not produce abundant flowers or fruit.

4) Wild vines climbed along the trunks and canopies of trees, and this constant upward growth diverted most of the vine's energy to making leaves instead of the orchid flowers that, once pollinated, would produce the flavorful pods.

5) Hundreds of years before vanilla became a prized food flavoring in Europe and the Western World, the Totonac Indians of the Mexican Gulf Coast were skilled cultivators of the vanilla vine, whose fruit they literally worshipped as a goddess.

The best order is

A. 2 3 4 1 5
B. 2 4 3 1 5
C. 5 3 4 2 1
D. 3 4 1 2 5

Group 7

1) Once airborne, the spider is at the mercy of the air currents—usually the spider takes a brief journey, traveling close to the ground, but some have been found in air samples collected as high as 10,000 feet, or been reported landing on ships far out at sea.

2) Once a young spider has hatched, it must leave the environment into which it was born as quickly as possible, in order to avoid competing with its hundreds of brothers and sisters for food.

3) The silk rises into warm air currents, and as soon as the pull feels adequate the spider lets go and drifts up into the air, suspended from the silk strand in the same way that a person might parasail.

4) To help young spiders do this, many species have adapted a practice known as "aerial dispersal," or, in common speech, "ballooning."

5) A spider that wants to leave its surroundings quickly will climb to the top of a grass stem or twig, face into the wind, and aim its back end into the air, releasing a long stream of silk from the glands near the tip of its abdomen.

The best order is

A.   5 4 2 3 1
B.   5 2 4 1 3
C.   2 5 4 3 1
D.   2 4 5 3 1

Group 8

1)   For about a year, Tycho worked at a castle in Prague with a scientist named Johannes Kepler, but their association was cut short by another argument that drove Kepler out of the castle, to later develop, on his own, the theory of planetary orbits.

2)   Tycho found life without a nose embarrassing, so he made a new nose for himself out of silver, which reportedly remained glued to his face for the rest of his life.

3)   Tycho Brahe, the 17th-century Danish astronomer, is today more famous for his odd and arrogant personality than for any contribution he has made to our knowledge of the stars and planets.

4)   Early in his career, as a student at Rostock University, Tycho got into an argument with the another student about who was the better mathematician, and the two became so angry that the argument turned into a sword fight, during which Tycho's nose was sliced off.

5)   Later in his life, Tycho's arrogance may have kept him from playing a part in one of the greatest astronomical discoveries in history: the elliptical orbits of the solar system's planets.

The best order is

A.   1 4 2 3 5
B.   4 2 3 5 1
C.   4 2 1 3 5
D.   3 4 2 5 1

Group 9

1)   The processionaries are so used to this routine that if a person picks up the end of a silk line and brings it back to the origin—creating a closed circle—the caterpillars may travel around and around for days, sometimes starving ar freezing, without changing course.

2)   Rather than relying on sight or sound, the other caterpillars, who are lined up end-to-end behind the leader, travel to and from their nests by walking on this silk line, and each will reinforce it by laying down its own marking line as it passes over.

3)   In order to insure the safety of individuals, the processionary caterpillar nests in a tree with dozens of other caterpillars, and at night, when it is safest, they all leave together in search of food.

4)   The processionary caterpillar of the European continent is a perfect illustration of how much some insect species rely on instinct in their daily routines.

5)   As they leave their nests, the processionaries form a single-file line behind a leader who spins and lays out a silk line to mark the chosen path.

The best order is

A.   4 3 5 2 1
B.   3 5 4 2 1
C.   3 5 2 1 4
D.   4 5 3 1 2

Group 10

1) Often, the child is also given a handcrafted walker or push cart, to provide support for its first upright explorations.

2) In traditional Indian families, a child's first steps are celebrated as a ceremonial event, rooted in ancient myth.

3) These carts are often intricately designed to resemble the chariot of Krishna, an important figure in Indian mythology.

4) The sound of these anklet bells is intended to mimic the footsteps of the legendary child Rama, who is celebrated in devotional songs throughout India.

5) When the child's parents see that the child is ready to begin walking, they will fit it with specially designed ankle bracelets, adorned with gently ringing bells.

The best order is

A.   2 3 4 1 5
B.   2 5 3 1 4
C.   5 4 1 3 2
D.   5 3 2 1 4

Group 11

1)   The settlers planted Osage orange all across Middle America, and today long lines and rectangles of Osage orange trees can still be seen on the prairies, running along the former boundaries of farms that no longer exist.

2)   After trying sod walls and water-filled ditches with no success, American farmers began to look for a plant that was adaptable to prairie weather, and that could be trimmed into a hedge that was "pig-tight, horse-high, and bull-strong."

3)   The tree, so named because it bore a large (but inedible) fruit the size of an orange, was among the sturdiest and hardiest of American trees, and was prized among Native Americans for the strength and flexibility of bows which were made from its wood.

4)   The first people to practice agriculture on the American flatlands were faced with an important problem: what would they use to fence their land in a place that was almost entirely without trees or rocks?

5)   Finally, an Illinois farmer brought the settlers a tree that was native to the land between the Red and Arkansas rivers, a tree called the Osage orange.

The best order is

A.   2 1 5 3 4
B.   1 2 3 4 5
C.   4 2 5 3 1
D.   4 2 1 3 5

Group 12

1)   After about ten minutes of such spirited and complicated activity, the head dancer is free to make up his or her own movements while maintaining the interest of the New Year's crowd.

2)   The dancer will then perform a series of leg kicks, while at the same time operating the lion's mouth with his own hand and moving the ears and eyes by means of a string which is attached to the dancer's own mouth.

3)   The most difficult role of this dance belongs to the one who controls the lion's head; this person must lead all the other "parts" of the lion through the choreographed segments of the dance.

4)   The head dancer begins with a complex series of steps, alternately stepping forward with the head raised, and then retreating a few steps while lowering the head, a movement that is intended to create the impression that the lion is keeping a watchful eye for anything evil.

5)   When performing a traditional Chinese New Year's lion dance, several performers must fit themselves inside a large lion costume and work together to enact different parts of the dance.

The best order is

A.   5 3 4 2 1
B.   3 4 2 5 1
C.   3 1 5 4 2
D.   4 2 3 5 1

Group 13

1)   For many years the shell of the chambered nautilus was treasured in Europe for its beauty and intricacy, but collectors were unaware that they were in possession of the structure that marked a "missing link" in the evolution of marine mollusks.

2)   The nautilus, however, evolved a series of enclosed chambers in its shell, and invented a new use for the structure: the shell began to serve as a buoyancy device.

3)   Equipped with this new flotation device, the nautilus did not need the single, muscular foot of its predecessors, but instead developed flaps, tentacles, and a gentle form of jet propulsion that transformed it into the first mollusk able to take command of its own destiny and explore a three-dimensional world.

4)   By pumping and adjusting air pressure into the chambers, the nautilus could spend the day resting on the bottom, and then rise toward the surface at night in search of food.

5)   The nautilus shell looks like a large snail shell, similar to those of its ancestors, who used their shells as protective coverings while they were anchored to the sea floor.

The best order is

A.   5 2 4 1 3
B.   5 1 2 3 4
C.   1 2 5 3 4
D.   1 5 2 4 3

Group 14

1) While France and England battled for control of the region, the Acadiens prospered on the fertile farmland, which was finally secured by England in 1713.

2) Early in the 17th century, settlers from western France founded a colony called Acadie in what is now the Canadian province of Nova Scotia.

3) At this time, English officials feared the presence of spies among the Acadiens who might be loyal to their French homeland, and the Acadiens were deported to spots along the Atlantic and Caribbean shores of America.

4) The French settlers remained on this land, under English rule, for around forty years, until the beginning of the French and Indian War, another conflict between France and England.

5) As the Acadien refugees drifted toward a final home in southern Louisiana, neighbors shortened their name to "'Cadien," and finally "Cajun," the name which the descendants of early Acadiens still call themselves.

The best order is

A.   1 4 2 3 5
B.   2 1 3 5 4
C.   2 1 4 3 5
D.   5 2 3 4 1

Group 15   15. _____

1)   Traditional households in the Eastern and Western regions of Africa
serve two meals a day—one at around noon, and the other in the evening.

2)   The starch is then used in the way that Americans might use a spoon,
to scoop up a portion of the main dish on the person's plate.

3)   The reason for the starch's inclusion in every meal has to do with taste
as well as nutrition; African food can be very spicy, and the starch is known to
cool the burning effect of the main dish.

4)   When serving these meals, the main dish is usually served on individual plates, and the starch is served on a communal plate, from which diners
break off a piece of bread or scoop rice or fufu in their fingers.

5)   The typical meals usually consist of a thick stew or soup as the main
course, and an accompanying starch—either bread, rice, or *fufu*, a starchy
grain paste similar in consistency to mashed potatoes.

The best order is

A.   5 2 3 4 1
B.   5 1 4 3 2
C.   1 4 5 3 2
D.   1 5 4 2 3

Group 16

1)   In the early days of the American Midwest, Indiana settlers sometimes came together to hold an event called an apple peeling, where neighboring settlers gathered at the homestead of a host family to help prepare the hosts' apple crop for cooking, canning, and making apple butter.

2)   At the beginning of the event, each peeler sat down in front of a ten- or twenty-gallon stone jar and was given a crock of apples and a paring knife.

3)   Once a peeler had finished with a crock, another was placed next to him; if the peeler was an unmarried man, he kept a strict count of the number of apples he had peeled, because the winner was allowed to kiss the girl of his choice.

4)   The peeling usually ended by 9:30 in the evening, when the neighbors gathered in the host family's parlor for a dance social.

5)   The apples were peeled, cored, and quartered, and then placed into the jar.

The best order is

A.   1 5 3 4 2
B.   2 5 3 4 1
C.   1 2 5 3 4
D.   2 1 5 4 3

Group 17

1) If your pet turtle is a land turtle and is native to temperate climates, it will stop eating some time in October, which should be your cue to prepare the turtle for hibernation.

2) The box should then be covered with a wire screen, which will protect the turtle from any rodents or predators that might want to take advantage of a motionless and helpless animal.

3) When your turtle hasn't eaten for a while and appears ready to hibernate, it should be moved to its winter quarters, most likely a cellar or garage, where the temperature should range between 40° and 45°F.

4) Instead of feeding the turtle, you should bathe it every day in warm water, to encourage the turtle to empty its intestines in preparation for its long winter sleep.

5) Here the turtle should be placed in a well-ventilated box whose bottom is covered with a moisture-absorbing layer of clay beads, and then filled three-fourths full with almost dry peat moss or wood chips, into which the turtle will burrow and sleep for several months.

The best order is

A.   1 4 3 5 2
B.   3 4 2 5 1
C.   3 2 4 1 5
D.   4 5 2 3 1

Group 18

1) Once he has reached the nest, the hunter uses two sturdy bamboo poles like huge chopsticks to pull the nest away from the mountainside, into a large basket that will be lowered to people waiting below.

2) The world's largest honeybees colonize the Nepalese mountainsides, building honeycombs as large as a person on sheer rock faces that are often hundreds of feet high.

3) In the remote mountain country of Nepal, a small band of "honey hunters" carry out a tradition so ancient that 10,000 year-old drawings of the practice have been found in the caves of Nepal.

4) To harvest the honey and beeswax from these combs, a honey hunter climbs above the nests, lowers a long bamboo-fiber ladder over the cliff, and then climbs down.

5) Throughout this dangerous practice, the hunter is stung repeatedly, and only the veterans, with skin that has been toughened over the years, are able to return from a hunt without the painful swelling caused by stings.

The best order is

A. 2 4 3 5 1
B. 2 4 1 5 3
C. 5 3 2 4 1
D. 3 2 4 1 5

Group 19

1)   After the Romans left Britain, there were relentless attacks on the islands from the barbarian tribes of northern Germany—the Angles, Saxons, and Jutes.

2)   As the empire weakened, Roman soldiers withdrew from Britain, leaving behind a country that continued to practice the Christian religion that had been introduced by the Romans.

3)   Early Latin writings tell of a Christian warrior named Arturius (Arthur, in English) who led the British citizens to defeat these barbarian invaders, and brought an extended period of peace to the lands of Britain.

4)   Long ago, the British Isles were part of the far-flung Roman Empire that extended across most of Europe and into Africa and Asia.

5)   The romantic legend of King Arthur and his knights of the Round Table, one of the most popular and widespread stories of all time, appears to have some foundation in history.
The best order is

A.   5 4 3 2 1
B.   5 4 2 1 3
C.   4 5 2 3 1
D.   4 3 2 1 5

Group 20   20. _____

1)   The cylinder was allowed to cool until it sould stand on its own, and
then it was cut from the tube and split down the side with a single straight cut.

2)   Nineteenth-century glassmakers, who had not yet discovered the
glazier's modern techniques for making panes of glass, had to create a method
for converting their blown glass into flat sheets.

3)   The bubble was then pierced at the end to make a hole that opened up
while the glassmaker gently spun it, creating a cylinder of glass.

4)   Turned on its side and laid on a conveyor belt, the cylinder was
strengthened, or tempered, by being heated again and cooled very slowly,
eventually flattening out into a single rectangular piece of glass.

5)   To do this, the glassmaker dipped the end of a long tube into melted
glass and blew into the other end of the tube, creating an expanding bubble of
glass.

The best order is

A.   2 5 3 4 1
B.   2 4 5 3 1
C.   3 5 2 4 1
D.   3 1 4 5 2

Group 21

1) The splints are almost always hidden, but horses are occasionally born whose splinted toes project from the leg on either side, just above the hoof.

2) The second and fourth toes remained, but shrank to thin splints of bone that fused invisibly to the horse's leg bone.

3) Horses are unique among mammals, having evolved feet that each end in what is essentially a single toe, capped by a large, sturdy hoof.

4) Julius Caesar, an emperor of ancient Rome, was said to have owned one of these three-toed horses, and considered it so special that he would not permit anyone else to ride it.

5) Though the horse's earlier ancestors possessed the traditional mammalian set of five toes on each foot, the horse has retained only its third toe; its first and fifth toes disappeared completely as the horse evolved.

The best order is

A.   3 5 2 1 4
B.   5 3 2 4 1
C.   3 2 5 1 4
D.   5 2 3 1 4

Group 22

1)   The new building materials—some of which are twenty feet long, and
weigh nearly six tons—were transported to Pohnpei on rafts, and were
brought into their present position by using hibiscus fiber ropes and leverage
to move the stone columns upward along the inclined trunks of coconut palm
trees.

2)   The ancestors built great fires to heat the stone, and then poured cool
seawater on the columns, which caused the stone to contract and split along
natural fracture lines.

3)   The now-abandoned enclave of Nan Madol, a group of 92 man-made
islands off the shore of the Micronesian island of Pohnpei, is estimated to
have been built around the year 500 A.D.

4)   The islanders say their ancestors quarried stone columns from a nearby
island, where large basalt columns were formed by the cooling of molten lava.

5)   The structures of Nan Madol are remarkable for the sheer size of some
of the stone "logs" or columns that were used to create the walls of the off-
shore community, and today anthropologists can only rely on the information
of existing local people for clues about how Nan Madol was built.

The best order is

A.   5 4 3 2 1
B.   5 3 1 4 2
C.   3 5 4 2 1
D.   3 1 4 2 5

Group 23

1) One of the most easily manipulated substances on earth, glass can be made into ceramic tiles that are composed of over 90% air.

2) NASA's space shuttles are the first spacecraft ever designed to leave and re-enter the earth's atmosphere while remaining intact.

3) These ceramic tiles are such effective insulators that when a tile emerges from the oven in which it was fired, it can be held safely in a person's hand by the edges while its interior still glows at a temperature well over 2000° F.

4) Eventually, the engineers were led to a material that is as old as our most ancient civilizations—glass.

5) Because the temperature during atmospheric re-entry is so incredibly hot, it took NASA's engineers some time to find a substance capable of protecting the shuttles.

The best order is

A.   5 2 1 3 4
B.   2 5 4 1 3
C.   2 3 1 2 5
D.   5 4 3 1 2

Group 24

1)   The secret to teaching any parakeet to talk is patience, and the under-standing that when a bird "talks," it is simply imitating what it hears, rather than putting ideas into words.

2)   You should stay just out of sight of the bird and repeat the phrase you want it to learn, for at least fifteen minutes every morning and evening.

3)   It is important to leave the bird without any words of encouragement or farewell; otherwise it might combine stray remarks or phrases, such as "Good night," with the phrase you are trying to teach it.

4)   For this reason, to train your bird to imitate your words you should keep it free of any distractions, especially other noises, while you are giving it "lessons."

5)   After your repetition, you should quietly leave the bird alone for a while, to think over what it has just heard.

The best order is

A.   1 4 2 5 3
B.   1 2 4 3 5
C.   3 2 1 5 4
D.   3 1 5 4 2

Group 25

1)   As a school approaches, fishermen from neighboring communities join their fishing boats together as a fleet, and string their gill nets together to make a huge fence that is held up by cork floats.

2)   At a signal from the party leaders, or *nakura*, the family members pound the sides of the boats or beat the water with long poles, creating a sudden and deafening noise.

3)   The fishermen work together to drag the trap into a half-circle that may reach 300 yards in diameter, and then the families move their boats to form the other half of the circle around the school of fish.

4)   The school of fish flee from the commotion into the awaiting trap, where a final wall of net is thrown over the open end of the half-circle, securing the day's haul.

5)   Indonesian people from the area around the Sulu islands live on the sea, in floating villages made of lashed-together or stilted homes, and make much of their living by fishing their home waters for migrating schools of snapper, scad, and other fish.

The best order is

A.   1 5 3 4 2
B.   1 2 4 3 5
C.   5 1 2 3 4
D.   5 1 3 2 4

———

KEY (CORRECT ANSWERS)

1. D
2. D
3. B
4. A
5. C

6. C
7. D
8. D
9. A
10. B

11. C
12. A
13. D
14. C
15. D

16. C
17. A
18. D
19. B
20. A

21. A
22. C
23. B
24. A
25. D

EXAMINATION SECTION
Preparing Written Material

Directions: Each short paragraph below is followed by four restatements or summaries of the information contained within it. Select the one that most completely and accurately restates the information or opinion given in the paragraph. *PRINT THE LETTER OF THE CORRECT ANSWER IN THE SPACE AT THE RIGHT.*

1)   India's night jasmine, or hurshinghar, is different from most flowering plants, in that its flowers are closed during the day, and open after dark. The scientific reason for this is probably that the plant has avoided competing with other flowers for pollinating insects and birds, and relies instead on the service of nocturnal bats that are drawn to the flower's nectar. According to an old Indian legend, however, the flowers sprouted from the funeral ashes of a beautiful young girl who had fallen hopelessly in love with the sun.

1. _____

A.   Despite the Indian legend that explains why the hurshinghar's flowers open at dusk, scientists believe it has to do with competition for available pollinators.
B.   The Indian hurshinghar's closure of its flowers during the day is due to a lack of available pollinators.
C.   The hurshinghar of India has evolved an unhealthy dependency on nocturnal bats.
D.   Like most myths, the Indian legend of the hurshinghar's night-flowering has been disproved by science.

2)   Charles Lindbergh's trans-Atlantic flight from New York to Paris made him an international hero in 1927, but he lived nearly another fifty years, and by most accounts they weren't terribly happy ones. The two greatest tragedies of his life—the 1932 kidnapping and murder of his oldest son, and an unshakeable reputation as a Nazi sympathizer during World War II—he blamed squarely on the rabid media hounds who stalked his every move.

2. _____

A.   Despite the fact that Charles Lindbergh had a hand in the two greatest tragedies of his life, he insisted on blaming the media for his problems.
B.   Charles Lindbergh lived a largely unhappy life after the glory of his 1927 trans-Atlantic flight, and he blamed his unhappiness on media attention.
C.   Charles Lindbergh's later life was marked by despair and disillusionment.
D.   Because of the rabid media attention sparked by Charles Lindbergh's 1927 trans-Atlantic flight, he would later consider it the last happy event of his life.

3)   The United States, one of the world's youngest nations in the early
nineteenth century, had yet to spread its wings in terms of foreign affairs,
preferring to remain isolated and opposed to meddling in the affairs of others.
But the fact remained that as a young nation situated on the opposite side of
the globe from Europe, Africa, and Asia, the United States had much work to
do in establishing relations with the rest of the world. So, too, as the European colonial powers continued to battle for influence in North and South
America, did the United States come to believe that it was proper for them to
keep these nations from encroaching into their sphere of influence.

A.   The roots of the Monroe Doctrine can be traced to the foreign policy
shift of the United States during the early nineteenth century.
B.   In the early nineteenth century, the United States shifted its foreign
policy to reflect a growing desire to actively protect its interests in the Western
Hemisphere.
C.   In the early nineteenth century, the United States was too young and
undeveloped to have devised much in the way of foreign policy.
D.   The United States adopted a more aggressive foreign policy in the
early nineteenth century in order to become a diplomatic player on the world
stage.

4)   Hertha Ayrton, a nineteenth-century Englishwoman, pursued a career
in science during a time when most women were not given the opportunity to
go to college. Her series of successes led to her induction into the Institution
of Electrical Engineers in 1899, when she was the first woman to receive this
professional honor. Her most noted accomplishment was the research and
invention of an anti-gas fan that the British War Office used in the trench
warfare of World War I.

A.   The British Army's success in World War I can be partly attributed to
Hertha Ayrton, a groundbreaking British scientist.
B.   Hertha Ayrton was the first woman to be inducted into the Institution
of Electrical Engineers.
C.   The injustices of nineteenth-century England were no match for the
brilliant mind of Hertha Ayrton.
D.   Hertha Ayrton defied the restrictions of her society by building a
successful scientific career.

3

5)   Scientists studying hyenas in Tanzania's Ngorongoro Crater have observed that hyena clans have evolved a system of territoriality that allows each clan a certain space to hunt within the 100-square-mile area. These territories are not marked by natural boundaries, but by droppings and excretions from the hyenas' scent glands. Usually, the hyenas take these boundary lines very seriously; some hyena clans have been observed abandoning their pursuit of certain prey after the prey has crossed into another territory, even though no members of the neighboring clan are anywhere in sight.

5. _____

A.   The hyenas of Ngorongoro Crater illustrate that the best way to peacefully coexist within a limited territory is to strictly delineate and defend territorial borders.
B.   While most territorial boundaries are marked using geographical features, the hyenas of Ngorongoro Crater have devised another method.
C.   The hyena clans of Ngorongoro Crater, in order to co-exist within a limited hunting territory, have developed a method of marking strict territorial boundaries.
D.   As with most species, the hyenas of Ngorongoro Crater have proven the age-old motto: "To the victor go the spoils."

6)   The flood control policy of the U.S. Army Corps of Engineers has long been an obvious feature of the American landscape—the Corps seeks to contain the nation's rivers with an enormous network of dams and levees, "channelizing" rivers into small, confined routes that will stay clear of settled floodplains when rivers rise. As a command of the U.S. Army, the Corps seems to have long seen the nation's rivers as an enemy to be fought; one of the agency's early training films speaks of the Corps' "battle" with its adversary, Mother Nature.

6. _____

A.   The dams and levees built by the U.S. Army Corps of Engineers have at least defeated their adversary, Mother Nature.
B.   The flood control policy of the U.S. Army Corps of Engineers has often reflected a military point of view, making the nation's rivers into enemies that must be defeated.
C.   When one realizes that the flood policy of the U.S. Army Corps of Engineers has always relied on a kind of military strategy, it is only possible to view the Corps' efforts as a failure.
D.   By damming and channelizing the nation's rivers, the U.S. Army Corps of Engineers have made America's floodplains safe for farming and development.

7)   Frogs with extra legs or missing legs have been showing up with   7. _____
greater frequency over the past decade, and scientists have been baffled by the
cause. Some researchers have concluded that pesticide runoff from farms is to
blame; others say a common parasite, the trematode, is the culprit. Now, a
new study suggests that both these factors in combination have disturbed
normal development in many frogs, leading to the abnormalities.

A.   Despite several studies, scientists still have no idea what is causing the
widespread incidence of deformities among aquatic frogs.
B.   In the debate over what is causing the increase in frog deformities,
environmentalists tend to blame pesticide runoff, while others blame a common parasite, the trematode.
C.   A recent study suggests that both pesticide runoff and natural parasites
have contributed to the increasing rate of deformities in frogs.
D.   Because of their aquatic habitat, frogs are among the most susceptible
organisms to chemical and environmental change, and this is illustrated by the
increasing rate of physical deformities among frog populations.

8)   The builders of the Egyptian pyramids, to insure that each massive   8. _____
structure was built on a completely flat surface, began by cutting a network of
criss-crossing channels into the pyramid's mapped-out ground space and
partly filling the channels with water. Because the channels were all interconnected, the water was distributed evenly throughout the channel system, and
all the workers had to do to level their building surface was cut away any rock
above the waterline.

A.   The modern carpenter's level uses a principle that was actually invented several centuries ago by the builders of the Egyptian pyramids.
B.   The discovery of the ancient Egyptians' sophisticated construction
techniques is a quiet argument against the idea that they were built by slaves.
C.   The use of water to insure that the pyramids were level mark the
Egyptians as one of the most scientifically advanced of the ancient civilizations.
D.   The builders of the Egyptian pyramids used a simple but ingenious
method for ensuring a level building surface with interconnected channels of
water.

9)   Thunderhead Mountain, a six-hundred-foot-high formation of granite   9. _____
in the Black Hills of South Dakota, is slowly undergoing a transformation that
will not be finished for more than a century, when what remains of the mountain will have become the largest sculpture in the world. The statue, begun in
1947 by a Boston sculptor named Henry Ziolkowski, is still being carved and
blasted by his wife and children into the likeness of Crazy Horse, the legendary chief of the Sioux tribe of American natives. The enormity of the sculpture—the planned length of one of the figure's arms is 263 feet—is under-
standable, given the historical greatness of Crazy Horse.

A.   Only a hero as great as Crazy Horse could warrant a sculpture so large
that it will take more than a century to complete.
B.   In 1947, sculptor Henry Ziolkowski began work on what he imagined
would be the largest sculpture in the world—even though he knew he would
not live to see it completed.
C.   The huge Black Hills sculpture of the great Sioux chief Crazy Horse,
still being carried out by the family of Henry Ziolkowski, will some day be
the largest sculpture in the world.
D.   South Dakota's Thunderhead Mountain will soon be the site of the
world's largest sculpture, a statue of the Sioux chief Crazy Horse.

10)   Because they were some of the first explorers to venture into the   10. _____
western frontier of North America, the French were responsible for the nam-
ing of several native tribes. Some of these names were poorly conceived—the
worst of which was perhaps Eskimo, the name for the natives of the far North,
which translates roughly as "eaters of raw flesh." The name is incorrect; these
people have always cooked their fish and game, and they now call themselves
the Inuit, a native term that means "the people."

A.   The first to explore much of North America's western frontier were the
French, and they usually gave improper or poorly-informed names to the
native tribes.
B.   The Eskimos of North America have never eaten raw flesh, so it is
curious that the French would give them a name that means "eaters of raw
flesh."
C.   The Inuit have fought for many years to overcome the impression that
they eat raw flesh.
D.   Like many native tribes, the Inuit were once incorrectly named by
French explorers, but they have since corrected the mistake themselves.

11)   Of the 30,000 species of spiders worldwide, only a handful are danger-   11. _____
ous to human beings, but this doesn't prevent many people from having a
powerful fear of all spiders, whether they are venomous or not. The leading
scientific theory about arachnophobia, as this fear is known, is that far in our
evolutionary past, some species of spider must have presented a serious
enough threat to people that the sight of a star-shaped body or an eight-legged
walk was coded into our genes as a danger signal.

A.   Scientists theorize that peoples' widespread fear of spiders can be
traced to an ancient spider species that was dangerous enough to trigger this
fearful reaction.
B.   The fear known as arachnophobia is triggered by the sight of a star-
shaped body or an eight-legged walk.
C.   Because most spiders have a uniquely shaped body that triggers a
human fear response, many humans are afflicted with the fear of spiders
known as arachnophobia.
D.   Though only a few of the planet's 30,000 spider species are dangerous
to people, many people have an unreasonable fear of them.

12)   From the 1970s to the 1990s, the percentage of Americans living in the   12. _____
suburbs climbed from 37% to 47%. In the latter part of the 1990s, a movement emerged that questioned the good of such a population shift—or at least,
the good of the speed and manner in which this suburban land was being
developed. Often, people began to argue, the planning of such growth was
flawed, resulting in a phenomenon that has become known as suburban
"sprawl," or the growth of suburban orbits around cities at rates faster than
infrastructures could support, and in ways that are damaging to the environment.

A.   The term "urban sprawl" was coined in the 1990s, when the movement
against unchecked suburban development began to gather momentum.
B.   In the 1980s and 1990s, home builders benefited from a boom in their
most favored demographic segment—suburban new-home buyers.
C.   Suburban development tends to suffer from poor planning, which can
lead to a lower quality of life for residents.
D.   The surge in suburban residences in the late twentieth century was
criticized by many as "sprawl" that could not be supported by existing resources.

13)   Medicare, a $200 billion-a-year program, processes 1 billion claims   13. _____
annually, and in the year 2000, the computer system that handles these claims
came under criticism. The General Accounting Office branded Medicare's
financial management system as outdated and inadequate—one in a series of
studies and reports warning that the program is plagued with duplication,
overcharges, double billings and confusion among users.

A.   The General Accounting Office's 2000 report proves that Medicare is a
bloated bureaucracy in need of substantial reform.
B.   Medicare's confusing computer network is an example of how the
federal government often neglects the programs that mean the most to average
American citizens.
C.   In the year 2000, the General Accounting Office criticized Medicare's
financial accounting network as inefficient and outdated.
D.   Because it has to handle so many claims each year, Medicare's financial accounting system often produces redundancies and errors.

14)   The earliest known writing materials were thin clay tablets, used in   14. _____
Mesopotamia more than 5,000 years ago. Although the tablets were cheap
and easy to produce, they had two major disadvantages: they were difficult to
store, and once the clay had dried and hardened a person could not write on
them. The ancient Egyptians later discovered a better writing material—the
thin bark of the papyrus reed, a plant that grew near the mouth of the Nile
River, which could be peeled into long strips, woven into a mat-like layer,
pounded flat with heavy mallets, and then dried in the sun.

A.   The Egyptians, after centuries of frustration with clay writing tablets,
were finally forced to invent a better writing surface.
B.   With the bark of the papyrus reed, ancient Egyptians made a writing
material that overcame the disadvantages of clay tablets.
C.   The Egyptian invention of the papyrus scroll was necessitated in part
by a relative lack of available clay.
D.   The word "paper" can be traced to the innovations of the Egyptians,
who made the first paper-like writing material from the bark of papyrus plant.

15)   In 1850, the German pianomaker Heinrich Steinweg and his family   15. _____
stepped off an immigrant ship in New York City, threw themselves into competition with dozens of other established craftsmen, and defeated them all by
reinventing the instrument. The company they created commanded the market
for nearly the next century and a half, while their competitors—some of the
most acclaimed pianomakers in the business—faded into obscurity. And all
the while, Steinway & Sons, through their sponsorship and encouragement of
the world's most distinguished pianists, helped define the cultural life of the
young United States.

A.   The Steinways capitalized on weak competition during the mid-
nineteenth century to capture the American piano market.
B.   Because of their technical and cultural innovations, the Steinways had
an advantage over other American pianomakers.
C.   Heinrich Steinweg founded the Steinway piano empire in 1850.
D.   From humble immigrant origins, the Steinway family rose to dominate
both the pianomaking industry and American musical culture.

16)   Feng Shui, the ancient Chinese science of studying the natural   16. _____
environment's effect on a person's well-being, has gained new popularity in
the design and decoration of buildings.
Although a complex area of study, a basic premise of Feng Shui is that each
building creates a unique field of energy which affects the inhabitants of that
building or home.
In recent years, decorators and realtors have begun to offer services which
include a diagnosis of a building's Feng Shui, or energy.

A.   Feng Shui, the Chinese science of balancing environmental energies,
has been given more aesthetic quality by recent practitioners.
B.   Generally, practitioners of Feng Shui work to create balance within a
room, carefully arranging sharp and soft surfaces to create a positive environment that suits the room's primary purpose.
C.   The idea behind the Chinese "science" of Feng Shui—that objects give
off certain energies that affect a building's inhabitants—has been a difficult
one for most Westerners to accept, but it is gaining in popularity.
D.   The ancient Chinese science of Feng Shui, which studies the balance
of energies in a person's environment, has become popular among those who
design and decorate buildings.

17)   Because the harsh seasonal variations of the Kansas plains make   17. _____
survival difficult for most plant life, the area is dominated by tall, sturdy
grasses. The only tree that has been able to survive—and prosper—throughout the wide expanse of prairie is the cottonwood, which can take root and
grow in the most extreme climatic conditions. Sometimes a storm will shear
off a living branch and carry it downstream, where it may snag along a sand-
bar and take root.

A.   Among the plant life of the Kansas plains, the only tree is the cottonwood.
B.   The only prosperous tree on the Kansas plains is the cottonwood,
which can take root and grow in a wide range of conditions.
C.   Only the cottonwood, whose branches can grow after being broken off
and washed down a river, is capable of surviving the climatic extremes of the
Kansas plains.
D.   Because it is the most widespread and hardiest tree on the Kansas
plains, the cottonwood had become a symbol of pioneer grit and fortitude.

18)   In the twenty-first century, it's easy to see the automobile as the key-   18. _____
stone of American popular culture. Subtract linen dusters, driving goggles,
and women's *crepe de chine* veils from our history, and you've taken the
Roaring out of the Twenties. Take away the ducktail haircuts, pegged pants
and upturned collars from the teen Car Cult of the Fifties, and the decade isn't
nearly as Fabulous. Were the chromed and tailfinned muscle cars of the
automobile's Golden Age modeled after us, or were we mimicking them?

A.   Ever since its invention, the automobile has shaped American culture.
B.   Many of the familiar names we give historical eras, such as "Roaring
Twenties" and "Fabulous Fifties," were given because of the predominance of
the automobile.
C.   Americans' tastes in clothing have been determined primarily by the
cars they drive.
D.   Teenagers have had a fascination for automobiles ever since the
motorcar was first invented.

19)   Since the 1960s, an important issue for Canada has been the status of   19. _____
minority French-speaking Canadians, especially in the province of Quebec,
whose inhabitants make up 30% of the Canadian population and trace their
ancestry back to a Canada that preceded British influence. In response to
pressure from Quebec nationalists, the government in 1982 added a Charter of
Rights to the constitution, restoring important rights that dated back to the
time of aboriginal treaties. Separatism is still a prominent issue, though
successive referendums and constitutional inquiries have not resulted in any
realistic progress toward Quebec's independence.

A.   Despite the fact that Quebec's inhabitants have their roots in Canada's
original settlers, they have been constantly oppressed by the descendants of
those who came later, the British.
B.   It seems unavoidable that Quebec's linguistic and cultural differences
with the rest of Canada will some day lead to its secession.
C.   French-speaking Quebec's activism over the last several decades has
led to concessions by the Canadian government, but it seems that Quebec will
remain a part of the country for some time.
D.   The inhabitants of Quebec are an aboriginal culture that has been
exploited by the Canadian government for years, but they are gradually
winning back their rights.

20)   For years, musicians and scientists have tried to discover what it is   20. _____
about an eighteenth-century Stradivarius violin—which may sell for more
than $1 million on today's market—that gives it its unique sound. In 1977,
American scientist Joseph Nagyvary discovered that the Stradivarius is made
of a spruce wood that came from Venice, where timber was stored beneath the
sea, and unlike the dry-seasoned wood from which other violins were made,
this spruce contains microscopic holes which add resonance to the violin's
sound. Nagyvary also found the varnish used on the Stradivarius to be equally
unique, containing tiny mineral crystals that appear to have come from
ground-up gemstones, which would filter out high-pitched tones and give the
violin a smoother sound.

A.   After carefully studying Stradivarius violins to discover the source of
their unique sound, an American scientist discovered two qualities in the
construction of them that set them apart from other instruments: the wood
from which they were made, and the varnish used to coat the wood.
B.   The two qualities that give the Stradivarius violin such a unique sound
are the wood, which adds resonance, and the finish, which filters out high-
pitched tones.
C.   The Stradivarius violin, because of the unique wood and finish used in
its construction, is widely regarded as the finest string instrument ever manu-
factured in the world.
D.   A close study of the Stradivarius violin has revealed that the best wood
for making violins is Venetian spruce, stored underwater.

21) People who watch the display of fireflies on a clear summer evening   21. _____
are actually witnessing a complex chemical reaction called "bioluminescence," which turns certain organisms into living light bulbs. Organisms that
produce this light undergo a reaction in which oxygen combines with a chemical called lucerfin and an enzyme called luciferase. Depending on the organ-
ism, the light produced from this reaction can range from the light green of the
firefly to the bright red spots of a railroad worm.

A.   Although the function of most displays of bioluminescence is to attract
mates, as is the case with fireflies, other species rely on bioluminescence for
different purposes.
B.   Bioluminescence, a phenomenon produced by several organisms, is
the result of a chemical reaction that takes place within the body of the organ-
ism.
C.   Of all the organisms in the world, only insects are capable of display-
ing bioluminescence.
D.   Despite the fact that some organisms display bioluminescence, these
reactions produce almost no heat, which is why the light they create is sometimes referred to as cold light.

22) The first of America's "log cabin" presidents, Andrew Jackson rose   22. _____
from humble backcountry origins to become a U.S. congressman and senator,
a renowned military hero, and the seventh president of the United States.
Among many Americans, especially those of the western frontier, he was
acclaimed as a symbol of the "new" American: self-made, strong through
closeness to nature, and endowed with a powerful moral courage.

A.   Andrew Jackson was the first American president to rise from modest
origins.
B.   Because he was born poor, President Andrew Jackson was more
popular among Americans of the western frontier.
C.   Andrew Jackson's humble background, along with his outstanding
achievements, made him into a symbol of American strength and self-suffi-
ciency.
D.   Andrew Jackson achieved success as a legislator, soldier, and president
because he was born humbly and had to work for every honor he ever received.

23)   In the past few decades, while much of the world's imagination has
focused on the possibilities of outer space, some scientists have been exploring a different frontier—the ocean floor. Although ships have been sailing the
oceans for centuries, only recently have scientists developed vehicles strong
enough to sustain the pressure of deep-sea exploration and observation. These
fiberglass vehicles, called submersibles, are usually just big enough to take
two or three people to the deepest parts of the oceans' floors.

23. _____

A.   Modern submersible vehicles, thanks to recent technological innovations, are now explore underwater cliffs, crevices and mountain ranges that
were once unreachable.
B.   While most people tend to fantasize about exploring outer space, they
should be turning toward a more accessible realm—the depths of the earth's
oceans.
C.   Because of the necessarily small size of submersible vehicles, exploration of the deep ocean is not a widespread activity.
D.   Recent technological developments have helped scientists to turn their
attention from deep space to the deep ocean.

24)   The panda—a native of the remote mountainous regions of China—
subsists almost entirely on the tender shoots of the bamboo plant. This restric-
tive diet has allowed the panda to evolve an anatomical structure that is
completely different from that of other bears, whose paws are aligned for
running, stabbing, and scratching. The panda's paw has an over-developed
wrist bone that juts out below the other claws like a thumb, and the panda uses
this "thumb" to grip bamboo shoots while it strips them of their leaves.

24. _____

A.   The panda is the only bear-like animal that feeds on vegetation, and it
has a kind of thumb to help it grip bamboo shoots.
B.   The panda's limited diet of bamboo has led it to evolve a thumb-like
appendage for grasping bamboo shoots.
C.   The panda's thumb-like appendage is a factor that limits its diet to the
shoots of the bamboo plant.
D.   Because bamboo shoots must be held tightly while eaten, the panda's
thumb-like appendage ensure that it is the only bear-like animal that eats
bamboo.

13

25) The stability and security of the Balkan region remains a primary
concern for Greece in post-Cold War Europe, and Greece's active participation in peacekeeping and humanitarian operations in Georgia, Albania, and
Bosnia are substantial examples of this commitment. Due to its geopolitical
position, Greece believes it necessary to maintain, at least for now, a more
nationalized defense force than other European nations. It is Greece's hope
that the new spirit of integration and cooperation will help establish a common
European foreign affairs and defense policy that might ease some of these
regional tensions, and allow a greater level of Greek participation in NATO's
integrated military structure.

25. _____

A.   Greece's proximity to the unstable Balkan region has led it to keep a
more nationalized military, though it hopes to become more involved in a
common European defense force.
B.   The Balkan states present a greater threat to Greece than any other
European nation, and Greece has adopted a highly nationalist military force as
a result.
C.   Greece, the only Balkan state to belong to NATO, has an isolationist
approach to defense, but hopes to achieve greater integration in the
organization's combined forces.
D.   Greece's failure to become more militarily integrated with the rest of
Europe can be attributed to the failure to establish a common European de-
fense policy.

KEY (CORRECT ANSWERS)

1. A
2. B
3. B
4. D
5. C

6. B
7. C
8. D
9. C
10. D

11. A
12. D
13. C
14. B
15. D

16. D
17. B
18. A
19. C
20. A

21. B
22. C
23. D
24. B
25. A

GLOSSARY OF MEDICAL INSURANCE TERMS

Advance Directives
Because of illness or injury, people are sometimes unable to talk to a doctor about treatment. Advance directives are written instructions that state a patient's wishes abut treatment in such instances before they happen.

Ambulatory Surgery
This is surgery that does not require inpatient hospital admission. It is also called one-day, same-day or *outpatient* surgery.

Appeal
A written or oral request from a member or provider to review and change a previous medical appropriateness (necessity) or experimental/investigational technology decision including denials requiring clinical expertise.

Behavioral Health Care Management Program
This program manages mental health and substance abuse care benefits. The behavioral health care management program must pre-approve and coordinate all mental health treatment and alcohol/substance abuse care. Your PCP's or personal physician's approval is not needed. Members must follow program requirements to receive benefits.

Benefits
These are the covered services available to a member. Your benefits are defined in your Certificate.

Certificate of Coverage (Certificate)
This is your evidence of health maintenance organization (HMO) coverage. Your Certificate provides the most detailed information about covered medical and hospital benefits.

Clinical Care, Decisions and Issues, Clinical Professionals and Clinical Reviews
Information relating to a patient's medical health and the status of the patient's medical health is a **clinical issue**. **Clinical care** is the medical treatment provided to the patient. A **clinical decision** is a decision given about a patient's medical treatment. Doctors and nurses as well as other health care professionals are **clinical professionals**. When doctors, nurses or other professionals review information about a patient's health, it is called a **clinical review**.

Complaint
This is a verbal or written statement of dissatisfaction where the insurance company is not being asked to review and overturn a previous determination.

Coordination of Benefits
This outlines how primary and secondary insurance providers coordinate payments and benefits when a claim is made, depending on which plan is primary or secondary and what their respective policies are.

Co-payment
This is your out-of-pocket payment for some services. For example, you must pay a specific dollar amount for each doctor's office visit; this is considered a co-payment.

Credentialing

This refers to reviewing the documentation of health care providers and determining if they meet a provider's network standards. Such documentation includes medical license, certifications, insurance and proof of malpractice insurance. Network physicians must pass the credentialing process every two years.

Custodial Care

This is care that mainly helps a person with daily activities, as defined by Medicare guidelines. It is care that does not need the supervision of trained medical or paramedical staff. It is not *skilled nursing care.* It generally does not cover such care that is primarily custodial such as: personal care that assists members with functions such as walking, getting in and out of bed, aid in bathing, dressing, feeding, toilet use, etc.; preparation of special diets; or giving medication that usually can be taken on one's own.

Diagnostic Procedures

This term refers to X-rays, lab tests, etc. ordered by a doctor to help identify a condition or disease and confirm a diagnosis.

Doctor

A doctor is a licensed doctor of medicine (M.D.) or a doctor of osteopathy (D.O.). Also called a physician.

Drug Formulary

This is a large list of medically appropriate, generic and brand-name medications for almost all conditions and situations. The list is reviewed and adjusted often. Network providers have this list, and are notified of any changes. You may obtain a copy by contacting your insurance company.

Elective Surgery

This is surgery done on a non-emergency basis.

Emergency Condition

An emergency condition is a medical or behavioral condition which affects you suddenly. It is accompanied by symptoms of such severity, including severe pain that a prudent lay person with an average knowledge of medicine and health could reasonably expect that the absence of immediate medical attention would:

- Place your health or, in the case of a behavioral condition, the health of others in serious jeopardy
- Cause serious impairment to bodily functions
- Cause serious dysfunction of any body organ or part
- Cause serious disfigurement

Exclusion

This is an element or service that a provider does not cover. See your Certificate for the exclusions and *limitations* that apply to your program.

Grievance

This is a written or oral request to review an adverse determination concerning an administrative decision not involving medical appropriateness (necessity).

Health Care Provider or Provider
This is a professionally licensed individual or entity giving health-related care to patients. Examples of providers include, but are not limited to: a physician, hospital, *skilled nursing facility*, pharmacy, *chiropractor*, nurse, nurse-midwife, physical therapist, speech pathologist, laboratory, etc. While all network providers are considered health care providers, *not all health care providers are network providers*. See **Network Provider** and **Non-Network Provider**.

Health Maintenance Organization (HMO)
An HMO provides comprehensive health care coverage to its members exclusively through a network of doctors, hospitals and other health care providers, with few co-payments.

Home Health Care
This is skilled nursing care and related services performed at a patient's home by a home health agency.

Hospice
This is a program that provides pain control and supportive care for *terminally ill* patients and their families. Hospice patients are not generally expected to survive more than six months.

Hospital
A fully licensed network hospital that has an agreement with insurance providers to provide services to covered persons under an HMO contract.

Inpatient
This term refers to a member who is admitted to and fills a bed in a network hospital or facility.

Limitation
This is a stipulation that specific services are covered only under certain conditions or for a designated number of times, days or visits within a given period. See your Certificate and Schedule of Benefits for more information about any limitations to your benefits.

Medical Management Program
Insurance companies work with your doctors to help ensure that you receive the right level of care. Your PCP or other network specialist must contact your insurance company for approval so that you receive maximum benefits. All network physicians are aware of their responsibility to contact the insurance provider.

Medically Necessary or Medical Necessity
Services, supplies or equipment provided by a hospital or other covered health care provider are generally considered medically necessary if it is determined that they are:

- Consistent with the symptoms or diagnosis and treatment of the patient's condition, illness or injury;
- In accordance with standards of good medical practice;
- Not solely for the convenience of the patient, family or provider;
- Not primarily custodial; and
- The most appropriate level of service for the patient's safety.

The fact that a network provider may have prescribed, recommended or approved a service, supply or equipment does not, in itself, make it medically necessary and appropriate.

Member
A member is a person, including eligible dependents, enrolled in an HMO.

Network Provider
This is a health care provider (i.e., physician, *skilled nursing facility*, home health agency, laboratory or pharmacy, etc.) who has an agreement with an insurance company to provide covered services to HMO members. Your ID card indicates the name of the network that your group selected.

Non-Network Provider
This is a health care provider (also known as an *out-of-network provider)* or hospital/facility that does not have an agreement.

One-Day Surgery
See **Ambulatory Surgery**

Outpatient
This term refers to services that a member may receive in a hospital or facility, but not as an admitted patient filling a bed.

Outpatient Surgery
See **Ambulatory Surgery**

Participating Provider
See **Network Provider**

Physician
See **Doctor**

Precertify/Precertification
This term means that Medical Management or behavioral health care management programs (when required) approved covered services. These approvals are generally required before you can receive care. This process is also referred to as "preauthorization" or "prior approval."

Primary Care Physician (PCP)
A PCP is the network physician – a family practitioner, general practitioner, internist or pediatrician (for children) – who is responsible for delivering or coordinating all your covered care. The only exceptions are:

- Behavioral health care that must be precertified, and
- Routine well woman care with a network obstetrician/gynecologist (OB/GYN).

Referral Care
This is covered care provided by a network provider (such as a *specialist*) *other than* your PCP.

Retrospective Review for Medical Necessity
This is a review performed after services are done (usually on a claim or appeal), that ensures that the care provided was consistent with the symptoms or diagnosis of the patient's condition. A review is also generally performed to see that the care was given in the right setting, by the appropriate, credentialed provider and in accordance with current, recognized standards of sound medical practice. See also **Appeal** and **Credentialing**.

Rider
A rider is a benefit purchased by your group that is not part of your basic coverage.

Same-Day Surgery
See **Ambulatory Surgery**

Schedule of Benefits
Attached to your Certificate, the Schedule defines obligations and benefits such as co-payments, age limits for children and items that are specific to your group's coverage.

Short-term
This term refers to treatment or care meant to improve or restore a member's functioning within a reasonable period of time. Short-term care is expected to have a positive result, not just maintain a member's level of functioning or prevent further decline.

Skilled Nursing Facility
This facility provides inpatient care for recovering patients who do not require acute hospital care, but do require medical services.

Specialty Care Center
This is a facility accredited or designated by a State agency or by a voluntary national health organization having special expertise in treating a specified condition or disease.

Specialist Care Coordinator
This is a network specialist with expertise in treating the member's disabling and degenerative or life-threatening disease or condition, which must require specialized medical care over a prolonged period of time. Insurance providers can arrange for a Specialist Care Coordinator to function as a PCP, if medically necessary.

Specialized Services
These are services provided by specialists other than your PCP. For example, an allergist (who treats allergies), a radiologist (who uses X-rays for diagnosis and treatment) and a *chiropractor* are specialists.

Urgent Care
This is timely medical treatment for a condition that is not a true medical emergency. For instance, urgent care could include treatment for bronchitis, nosebleeds, high fever or a sprained ankle. When you have an urgent care situation, call your personal physician or PCP. See **Emergency** for a definition of medical conditions that are true emergencies.